THE AKRON ANTHOLOGY

Edited by Jason Segedy
Introduction by David Giffels

First edition 2016

ISBN: 978-0-9968367-3-9

Belt Publishing
1667 E. 40th Street #1G1
Cleveland, Ohio 44120
www.beltmag.com

Book design by David Wilson

Also from Belt Publishing

Happy Anyway: A Flint Anthology
Cleveland Neighborhood Guidebook
How to Live in Detroit Without Being a Jackass
The Pittsburgh Anthology
Car Bombs to Cookie Tables: The Youngstown Anthology
A Detroit Anthology
The Cincinnati Anthology
The Cleveland Anthology

TABLE OF CONTENTS

NOTE FROM THE EDITOR

The Akron Anthology would not be possible without the contributions of a great many committed and talented people.

I would like to thank Anne Trubek, founder and publisher of *Belt Publishing*, for adding Akron to her growing and highly acclaimed collection of city-themed anthologies. We in Akron truly appreciate the opportunity to lend our literary voices to the growing chorus of writers who are penning pieces that focus on the oft-overlooked cities of the so-called "Rust Belt."

A special thanks, as well, to Joanna Richards, copy editor, and Martha Bayne, editor-in-chief of *Belt Magazine*, who both did yeoman's work on the assembly, curation, and honing of the pieces that comprise this collection.

I would like to thank each of the writers featured in this collection for their willingness to offer a privileged glimpse into their hearts and souls, and into this sometimes fabulous, sometimes frustrating, always fascinating city that we love dearly. A special shout-out to David Giffels and Rita Dove, for their generosity with both their talent and their time.

Finally, I would like to thank the people of Akron: past, present, and future; famous and obscure. You range from Colonel Simon Perkins to F.A. Seiberling to LeBron James, and include the untold and unsung hundreds of thousands of people who have made this quirky and gritty city a wonderful place to call home. The stories that are told within these pages represent a small, yet mighty, portion of our collective story.

To all of you, who understand, without having to be told, the meaning of words and phrases like "Cadillac Hill," "Galley Boy," "devil strip," "JoJo," and "down in the valley"; to you, who know the difference between the "Innerbelt" and the "Interbelt." It is for you that we write this book. As David Giffels so poignantly states: "We are the stories we tell."

Indeed.

Best,
Jason Segedy, editor
Akron, Ohio

HERE ON THE GROUND:

AN INTRODUCTION

By David Giffels

There'd better be a blimp in here. Seriously: if there is not a blimp in this book, I'm going to return it to the library I stole it from. Right now, I'm like you, Dear Reader. I haven't read this book yet. I don't know what's in it. We're both here at the beginning. I know what I want. You know what you want.

I want a blimp.

Really, it would be absurd for an anthology of writing about Akron, Ohio, not to include a blimp. It's our St. Louis Arch, our Golden Gate Bridge.

Then again, the notion of "an anthology of writing about Akron, Ohio" itself seems pretty absurd.

Then again, so does a blimp.

But here we are, at the beginning of that very book. And I can't help but wonder what will be in here. It's important, this book. If you're reading this in, say, Tampa, or Frankfurt, or Middle-earth, you may want an explanation for that statement. Akron hardly seems worthy of so many bound pages, and the idea of those pages as "important" does require some explaining.

But that's OK, because one thing we're particularly good at is explaining ourselves. We do it all the time. We're like those Whos on Horton's clover, calling to the world, "We are here!" We have a healthy neurosis, and a Midwestern instinct toward helpfulness. We live in a place that's used to being anonymous, unnoticed, sometimes degraded, not often celebrated. We live in a place that *The American Mercury* magazine, back in 1926, described as "unbeautiful." I've never been able to find a better word than that for this place I love more than any other place. "Unbeautiful" doesn't mean "ugly." It describes something that is decidedly not beautiful (even though it is sometimes) and doesn't need to be (even though it does sometimes).

Is there anything more unbeautiful than the Goodyear blimp? Gray, looming, utilitarian—and yet its sight overhead evokes such a powerful response. Goose bumps, even. Its sheer size, its odd grace, its otherworldliness, its uncanny hover, its evocation of long-ago disasters—it brings the same chill that transcendent architecture brings, the spontaneous yet inscrutable appreciation for art in service of function.

Who among us fortunate enough to have been children here—here: the home not just of blimps, but of the All-American Soap Box Derby, the world's greatest basketball player, the alleged birthplace of the hamburger, the uncontested birthplace of the Dum Dum sucker; a children's paradise—who does not recall the automatic response to hearing that distant unmistakable drone? Bolt from the house to the outdoors, head craned upward, breath quickening, watching for it to appear above the treetops, a gray whale, gently bobbing on the windstream. Who among us as adults does not do the same, no matter how many dozens, how many hundreds of times we've experienced it? Who among us does not instinctively wave? And who among us does not believe that the blimp, in its own way, waves back?

It's a feeling almost all of us know, but also a feeling we know that no other place can quite understand. So we explain. And we explain. And we explain. We explain the weirdness that comes from a town steeped in oddball invention, a place unduly proud of its role in perfecting polyvinyl chloride and the Echoplex and the bias-ply tire. We explain the paradox of life in a postindustrial city surrounded by a national park. We explain pop music's brief fascination with something called "the Akron Sound." We explain our need to be distinct from our big brother Cleveland, and we explain why that is so important.

Therefore we are storytellers, by instinct and necessity. We know that we are descended from the best of times—a century ago Akron was the fastest growing city in America—and the worst of times. A generation ago Akron was the first notch in the Rust Belt. And these are stories to tell. We tell them because they have substance: the tales of a great rise and a great fall and a gritty fight back toward grace. And because they are not well known beyond our own borders.

That's why the stories in this book are important, because when stories are shared, they give our lives meaning and they give our lives dignity: "We are here, we are here." Sometimes we need to be heard together, in a chorus such as those collected in these pages.

I lied a little bit before when I said I didn't know what was in these pages. I peeked. (Spoiler alert: It's good. You should definitely read it.) The stories told here reveal a city's rich, mysterious, odd-leaning inner life, one that many of us will recognize but that the larger world might never have imagined. They capture our punk rock anti-glamour. They celebrate an unbeautiful place.

State Representative Emilia Sykes tells of seeking her somewhere-over-the-rainbow and finding it back home in Akron. Andrew Poulsen enters a guitar nerd's Wonka World behind the nondescript exterior of EarthQuaker Devices. L.S. Quinn leads us back into the old downtown hobbit hole of Mr. Bilbo's bar. Kyle Cochrun pulls us up to the tragic midnight rooftop of the abandoned Atlantic Foundry building. Jeff Shearl takes us into the backstage strangeness of E.J. Thomas Hall. And Jason Segedy gives voice to the Generation X experience of growing up in a postindustrial netherworld and seeing not the end of things, but new beginnings.

Archie the Snowman, the Black Keys, the Capital of West Virginia—these pieces of ourselves are arranged together here, each an offering from a single voice with something to say.

We are small here on the ground. We know this, because of the blimp. So we put our voices together.

But here on the ground, have you noticed it? That nagging silence? That thing that's not there?

When was the last time you heard the blimp overhead? A year? Two?

It's a little unnerving to those of us who've known that sound for so long, who've taken such pleasure and pride in it. For every other place in the world, the appearance of the Goodyear blimp means something epic—the Super Bowl, the World Series. For those of us who are neighbors to the Wingfoot Lake home base, the arrival of the blimp means it's a random Wednesday in Akron. A homely comfort. But lately, there's a void.

In 2014, Goodyear launched a new blimp, dubbed the "NT" (for "New Technology"), whose advances included a much quieter engine than the one that produced that telltale drone. The blimp, among many other things, has for a century been a reliable touchstone while also charting a metaphor of progress, growing from war machine to advertising balloon to living representation of Goodyear's drive for innovation.

I came to understand this lineage when I was working as a reporter for the *Akron Beacon Journal*. I used to find any excuse I could to go hang out at the Wingfoot Lake hangar. It was there I discovered something like what is revealed in this anthology—the stories behind the stories. For all the mechanical sophistication and corporate importance and stately history of Goodyear's airship program, the back end of that hangar was far more reminiscent of a mom-and-pop garage. A stained pot of bad coffee, spare parts cluttering the corners, the scent of welding sparks and machine oil, and a fellowship of old guys who call themselves "Helium Heads," spinning yarns. Much of the expertise of this strange Akron venture was passed down by the generation that built and operated and repaired the ships during World War II and the decades following. Much of the larger understanding of what these things mean and why they matter was preserved and passed on and most likely embellished across the worn break-room table next to the mechanic's area.

Even if I don't hear the blimp's arrival the way I once did, I still hear those voices—Jack LaFontaine, Joan Reisig, Ren Brown—and the joy they took in sharing the stories with me. Jack took me back into the dusty warehouse space one day and showed me a coffin packed in a wooden crate, stored there since the days when the Wingfoot Lake facility was used as a production factory for all sorts of government contracts. Joan told me the story of the out-of-service blimp gondola stored at a rear corner of the wide-open hangar—a piece of Goodyear's fabled "ghost ship," which took off one day with a two-man crew and later floated back to the ground, empty. Ren—who died just as this anthology was being completed—and I talked frequently about his tireless historical preservation work for the Lighter-Than-Air Society.

They, as much as anyone I've ever known, explain why the stories of a place are so important. We are here, they say. We are the stories we tell.

"WHEN ARE YOU COMING HOME?"

By Pat Jarrett

I find that a lot of photographers see Ohio as an endless sea of dead malls and salt-crusted cars on fire in front of rusted-out steel plants. It's more than that. The Ohio I know is tough and unforgiving. I never got a trophy for participation. I was never told that I was any more special than anyone else. The Ohio I know chews you up early so that when the shit hits the fan it's not as bad as it could have been—and as I grow older I'm thankful for that scar tissue.

The Ohio I know is full of the best friends anyone could ask for. Ohio friends are friends for life. Sure, we have our disagreements and maybe we fought on the playground in the fourth grade, but after thirty years I know I can count on my Ohio friends. They are bedrock. They are the friends who will make sure you aren't making a terrible decision. They will laugh at you right before they reach down to pick you up and dust you off and buy you a beer. They will fight anyone who means to hurt you.

I started this project when my maternal grandmother died. I continued to document through her husband's (my grandfather's) death, his funeral and the selling of his home in Stow that he bought when he came back from WWII. I photographed the loss of other family members, the return of my sister to Akron from Portland, Oregon, the birth of my nephew and the struggles of my family and friends.

Northeast Ohio doesn't have the luxury of a geographical crown jewel. No ocean or mountain range, no grand desert or majestic vistas really to speak of. Ohio's color palette is a shade above grey most of the year, and then there's construction and humidity. Because of this I feel like the people there really have to lock arms, look each other in the eye squarely and go on.

This body of work was inspired by my leaving northeast Ohio and the question I have been asked since I left, "When are you coming home?"

It was weird to see Grandpa in a wheelchair. He was constantly in and out of rehabilitation homes; this time was after he fell and fractured his back before his birthday in 2008. He was always so tall to me, and the older he got the smaller he seemed, even though he was still nearly six feet tall. I remember saying that he was as tall as a refrigerator to my friends. His daughter Kathy kisses his cheek after a picnic lunch at the rehabilitation home. August, 2008.

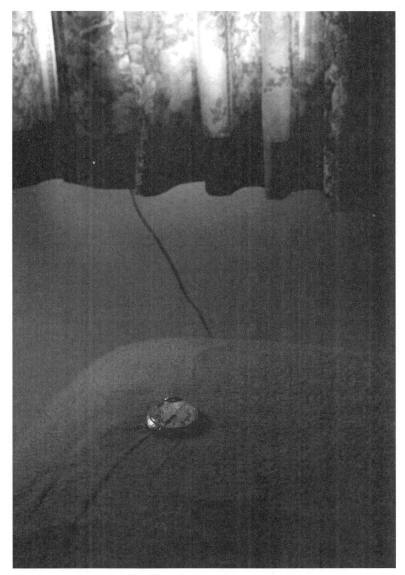

After my grandpa died my mother and aunt told me to go through the house and see what I wanted of his. I really didn't want anything; as much as I loved the man the only thing we had in common was shirt and suit size, so I planned to grab a few good work shirts. I always remember him in crisp, collared work shirts and suspenders, but they said I should have his pocket watch. Engraved on the back of the watch is a steam train, worn down to the bare metal from use. Here it is, on the electric blanket on the bed in his house in Stow, Ohio, April 2014.

A group of Grandpa Harry's nephews carry his flag-draped casket out of Holy Family Catholic Church in Stow, Ohio. Harry Tighe, my grandfather, died late on Monday, March 17, 2014 in Kent, Ohio, several miles from his home in Stow. Friday, March 20 family and friends carried his body to Oakwood Cemetery in Cuyahoga Falls, where his wife Ruth Ann is buried. March, 2014.

Shadow of a family portrait, Grandpa's house, Stow, Ohio, April 2014.

This is the street where I grew up. I lived across the street from two brothers who were merciless bullies, but still wanted to come over to my house to swim in our above-ground pool. I invited them over, for some reason, and never felt more uncomfortable. Uniondale Drive, Stow, Ohio, April, 2014.

Andy and I grew up one block from each other. I don't remember meeting Andy, that's how long we've been friends. As we've grown up we've dealt with issues with the frankness that comes with blood relation, though we aren't. I still feel regret about putting him in a headlock on the playground in third grade to look cool in front of popular kids. Camping, March 2016.

The Independence Day parade in Stow, Ohio, 2014.

Mom made Southern Comfort Punch for the July 4 parade using the leftover liquor she took from my Grandfather's house. I never saw Grandpa drink liquor, but he would drink Natural Light or Coors Original. The punch tasted like his house smelled, a bit sweet and thick with notes of Pine Sol.

Memorial Parkway near the Little Cuyahoga River in Akron, Ohio, July 2014.

Grandpa Harry's basement work bench in Stow, Ohio, April, 2014. His house sold in days after his death.

My mother kicked my sister's husband in the shin when he told her they were moving across the country. They lived on the west coast for a couple of years before having my nephew. Not long after, they decided to move back to Northeast Ohio to raise their son. My mother hung my sister's childhood bathing suit in the basement under a photograph of her wearing it. Through all the years of asking me when I was coming home, my sister ended up coming home first. She lived with her husband and son in this basement while they looked for a home.

Screaming nephew, summer 2015.

A TAVERN IN THE SHIRE

By L.S. Quinn

In the movies, hobbits have it pretty good. Peter Jackson's Bilbo Baggins lives in a flagstone-floored, beeswax-polished cottage in the Cotswolds, and it just happens to be underground. You can smell the lemon oil and pipe tobacco just looking at the screen. The Shire is filled with birdsong and sunlight, cows lowing on their way home from the pasture, hairy-footed hobbits folk-dancing in the grass.

But in my junior and senior years at the University of Akron, I worked in a real hobbit hole: Mr. Bilbo's, at 207 South Main Street. Just down the hill from campus and the now-defunct Inventors Hall of Fame, it was a low, half-timbered building, dark all day long and filthy. The walls were filled with paintings copied from the 1977 animated version of *The Hobbit*, coated in cigarette tar and half an inch of dust. We were extremely proud of those paintings, because they were Art.

The patrons were also dark and filthy. Cam was a stocky, bearded, leather-vested Mayflower Manor resident, who came in every day at exactly 4:37 to play "Low Rider" on the jukebox and get quietly drunk on $1.25 Buds. Every single day. I still flinch when the drummer starts hitting that cowbell.

Libby lived in a Communist homeless shelter and came in on Tuesdays to have the $2.75 grilled cheese sandwich and chicken velvet soup lunch special. She was always a bit twitchy. It turned out to be scabies. Tiny mites digging aimless patterns under her skin, leaving her endlessly scratching.

On Thursdays, a loud and loutish bunch of historic re-enactors would come in from their illicit practice on the UA soccer field to drink water, not tip, and creep on the female staff. They fit right in, in a hobbit-themed bar, with their fake swords and shields, their medieval-level filthiness. The women with cloaks made from Salvation Army fur, moth-chewed and shredding at the seams; the men in secondhand scrubs decorated with made-up coats of arms. One would pull out a pair of needle-nose pliers and start knitting homemade chain mail; another would order a single plate of wings for eighteen people to share. They smelled of cigarettes, old sweat, and unwashed laundry. They loved the past, but they loved Guinness, pot, and violence a lot more.

But Mark was a unique kind of dirty. We actually wouldn't let Mark past the doormat. He would come in, knee-deep in mud, carrying a shovel and a five-gallon bucket, and mutter, "Gmmmbrz," which meant, "A bottle of Guinness, in a paper bag, please." He had streaks of reddish mud up and down his shirt and caked over his forearms, and he smelled like stagnant water. We never knew where he came from or what cave he took that bottle to when he left.

Most of this clientele did not tip lavishly. Working a weekday afternoon, I might make eight dollars. Or three. Or negative forty (wage theft—credit card tips are easy for managers to make off with). Mostly I sat around drawing endlessly repeating patterns on my order pad. Occasionally a random patron would tip me something truly heartwarming, like a coaster with an obscene drawing, or a homemade suede flogger. The one guy I gave my number to at Mr. Bilbo's told me he liked golden showers on our first and only date.

But one day Mark sort of ducked his head and half-smiled as I handed him his paper bag of Guinness, and pulled another brown paper lunch bag out of his backpack. "Ibrotchusmthin." The bag was heavy—very heavy—and, like Mark, very dirty. I took it, somewhat gingerly, and unrolled the top to find the gleam of still-wet, freshly washed porcelain.

"I'm an archaeologist," Mark said. "Archaeologist" was the first fully formed word I'd ever heard him say. "I dig in the canal bed, under the Civic Theatre. We used to be the toy capital of the world."

"Did we?" I said, distracted, poking through the bag. I shook the clinking porcelain pieces out onto my cork tray: clean, white, delicately articulated porcelain doll parts. Feet, hands, and a couple of tiny broken heads; a few terra-cotta pitchers; half a blue-and-white painted willowware doll plate; some clay marbles. There were dozens of disembodied feet, an inch or so long, with tiny toes and curved ankles. Most were damaged, missing a bit of heel or toe, with a sharp, broken ankle or a chip out of the metatarsals.

"These are amazing! When are they from?"

"Eighteen-eighties-ish. They're maybe four feet down."

I rolled one of the marbles around the tray; it veered crazily around the edge, the line disrupted by the chips in its sides. Mark picked up the blue and white plate, his fingers leaving a streak of mud. "We used to be the glass capital of the world, too. There's good clay here, just a few feet under the surface. And children's books; Saalfield used to be the biggest publisher of children's books in the world. Horatio Alger, P.T. Barnum, Daniel Defoe. Beautiful lithographs. They ground the stones down after each book, though, so they're irreplaceable. Rubber isn't the only thing we've ever made."

The bartender came over, and we slid the tray onto the bar so Cam could see too. We picked up the clay pieces and set them down, weighed them, fingered the broken edges. There was a tiny ring carved around each ankle and wrist, to fasten the limbs. Looking at them, you thought not about the women sitting in sweatshops sewing cotton bodies, but about little girls' Christmases and birthdays, dolls being hugged, danced with, taken out for tea. That's what you thought about.

Everyone thinks about before. Before the plants closed, before the people left, before the university started the world's first corrosion engineering institute. We have plenty of rust around to study. There's no shortage of falling-down bridges, crumbling concrete, exposed rebar. But we used to make more than rubber and rust. We made books, and toys, and pottery. And doll feet. Tiny, beautiful, creepy white porcelain doll feet. Here in the Shire.

SIMPLE NEEDS

By Greg Milo

We're driving a van alongside the railroad tracks that run through Akron, Ohio. I'm up front. Another teacher, Jason, drives. Behind us are eight Hoban High School students, ranging from freshman to senior. Some have been out with us on a Wednesday night before, some are clueless first timers.

We pass the bus transit and keep bouncing along the rocky road that follows the tracks.

Every Wednesday, for seven years, we've headed out onto the streets, stopped in the alleys, trekked through the woods, and ridden along the rails of Akron with the purpose of seeing the faces of the city's growing homeless population.

We meet a lot of old and new friends out there. Our students learn names and humanity, opening their eyes to the existence of the poor and vulnerable. For a moment, people who are used to being looked through become visible. They receive a smile, not judgment. They can step out from behind their defenses and take a break from their struggle. For a moment they shed the simple label of "homeless," and along with it the prevailing ignorance that drives negative misperceptions.

But Project HOPE has another, equally important, purpose. It places our students into the action, where they escape the sometimes stifling constraints of four walls, bulletin boards and textbooks. Here the students learn by engaging and being present. There's no room for passive attendance or dismissive prejudice.

Tonight, we have once again prepared food and positivity, stuffing it in the back of our van, and less fortunate Akronites are waiting.

I receive a text on my phone from a couple wondering if we're planning on visiting their location tonight. I shoot back a message of uncertainty. There are hundreds of people on the streets, both part-time and full, and we can't hit everyone every night.

The veteran students in the back of the van ask about our friends.

"Are we going to see Billy?"

"Have you seen Adam for a while?

"What's the name of that one guy with the broken foot under

the bridge?"

"Get a bag together!" Jason interrupts, as he spots a man waving us down.

"What's going on, man?" Jason greets our buddy Chris. "You want some food?"

"Man, I'll take a bus pass, if you got one," Chris says, shaking his head, clearly frustrated.

There's not much more valuable on the streets of Akron than an all-day bus pass. These golden tickets are free rides to a job interview, a doctor's appointment, or to the VA.

Jason pulls a bus pass from his pocket and hands it to an enlivened Chris.

"Thanks, man." Chris stuffs the ticket away. "You got any batteries?"

"No. What kind do you need?" Jason asks.

"Double A."

Jason yells back to the students to write this information down in the scribe book.

"How's Susan?" Jason asks Chris.

"Man, don't ask," Chris says, his mouth contorting.

"Sore subject, eh?" I laugh.

"I'll see you guys later," Chris says, shaking Jason's hand.

We drive on.

"There's Jessica," Jason notices, and he pulls the van into the parking lot between the Akron Art Museum and the Summit Artspace. "I'll stay here with some kids to get some bags ready for the next stop."

I take the rest of the kids across the street to see Jessica.

She's been flying a sign on the corner of Broadway and Market Street since seven this morning. Her short sleeves are rolled up over her shoulders, and she wears dark glasses to save her eyes from the summer sun, which has given her exposed skin a look of leather, like a cowboy's face on the wind-swept plains of the West.

Jessica pulls her sunglasses onto her head as we approach. Her eyes shine vividly against her browned skin, almost reaching from their sockets, and a certain human connection grabs me.

She smiles, and any apprehension we might have had drains away.

Jessica is young, mid-twenties. Over the seven years of hanging out with people on the streets, in the woods, along the tracks, and in the alleys, I've noticed a growing number of people who I qualify as young—some just out of high school, some I could have taught during my thirteen years of teaching.

"I haven't had any coffee yet today," Jessica says. It's mid-afternoon, and I think about how completely useless I am without a few cups of coffee in the morning. Of all the horrific things I've heard about during my time with Project HOPE, this one simple need for coffee is as difficult to comprehend as any.

"We can grab you a cup, if you want," I offer. The students agree.

"No, that's okay," Jessica says. "Pretty soon Dave will come and give me a break. Then I'll walk down to Speedway."

She goes on to explain how she is particular about the amount of sugar and powdered cream. It has to be just right.

"I completely understand," I say. I tell Jessica and the students about the undrinkable coffee offered by the school in the teachers' lounge. "I have to bring my own, or it's not worth it."

"Exactly," Jessica agrees.

This cup of coffee is Jessica's one daily treat. It keeps her going. It gives her relief in an otherwise brutal situation.

"Oh, man. We've been at each other's throats recently," she says of her relationship with her husband Dave, shaking her head as she reflects.

The restless nights, the lack of opportunities, the dwindling hope, and the grappling with reality weighs heavy on Jessica and Dave. She feels stressed and admits she's resorting to fighting and yelling more often than before.

"Dave's out working an odd job he managed to find," Jessica says, and I can tell she enjoys telling us.

As she talks, I watch her teeth, which seem desperate to hang on for life. Some discolored, some crooked, a couple gone.

Jessica, like so many other people we talk to during our Project

HOPE Wednesdays, enjoys the conversation. She enjoys being recognized, called by name, and given attention, without judgment.

I hand Jessica a couple of all-day bus passes.

"Can I ask how you and Dave got to this point?" I inquire. I feel I know Jessica well enough by now that I can drop the question. "You guys get laid off?"

She tells me about how Dave had a good job working at his father's painting business. When the recession hit, the business struggled. Stress levels rose, and tension between father and son led to a falling out. It's a story I've heard before.

Without a steady income, Jessica and Dave decided to rent out a couple rooms at their house in North Hill.

"We should have known better," Jessica says, referring to her friends who skipped on paying the rent. "We shouldn't have trusted them." Jessica shakes her head. "I loved that house," she adds.

Over the years, I have found that having family support is one of the keys to staying off the streets. In the case of Jessica and Dave, they lost that support and ended up roaming from campsite to campsite and house to house, forced to fly a sign for money.

Despite the hardship, Jessica smiles and laughs a lot. Her blue eyes shine in the sun. She moved to Akron from Erie, PA, where I lived for a year. She lived on Sixth Street at the same time I lived on Fourth. She would have been a little girl at that time, playing in the relentless Erie winter snow, innocent to the unforgiving realities that plague her today.

We were all innocent children at one time. Cute and energetic kids who gave passing adults joy. I think about this fact often. The child versions of us have no clue what is in store, and nobody yet has any negative views about us.

But now, as the older Jessica stands on the corner, looking for some help, there are people who ignore her and think poorly of her for simply being who she is.

And all she wants is a cup of coffee.

Once again, we leave her to stand on the corner alone. We turn and wave as we cross Broadway. She smiles and waves back.

"Thank you," she says.

"See you later," I shout, knowing that I'll see her in the same place next week, but wishing she wouldn't be there, saved by some miracle and a cup of Speedway coffee.

Jason's waiting with the van running. He and his crew of students have bagged some food in preparation for a trip into the woods.

"People really live in here?" a student asks as we follow a primitive trail through a wooded area not too far from the life of downtown Akron.

The people living in tents prefer this rugged freedom to what they feel are unrealistic requirements of the shelter. In this wooded area, and surrounding ones, our friends are close to the necessities, such as food, water, and, of course, the holy library, where men and women can find refuge in a book or online.

We come across an opening. Several tents circle around a central fire pit. A couch sits under a tarp acting as an overhang. A plastic patio chair sits next to a makeshift end table. A cooler sits closed with a large rock on top—a raccoon security system, which I hear isn't a sure thing.

We stand with bags of food in our hands and some bottled water, but the residents aren't in.

A student kicks at the end table.

"Hey!" Jason calls to the student. "This is someone's home. Let's be respectful.

"Here comes someone now," a student notices.

A man not much older than our students makes his way from the opposite direction from which we walked.

He's shirtless, and there's a tattoo looping across his belly. The script makes it difficult to read, but it looks like it says "redneck."

"Hey, man, you hungry any?" I ask.

"Sure, dude, and I'll definitely take some of that water y'all have," he says.

We come to find Johnny is only twenty years old. He spent most of his day waiting for a temporary job, but the walk to the temp agency means he wakes at 3:00 a.m. to make sure he gets a good spot, but even then, he might sit waiting for hours. He was able to work for a few hours, but most of his time was spent doing nothing.

"Makes more sense to fly a sign," Johnny confesses, "but I won't do that."

"Why not?" a student asks.

Johnny doesn't have an answer. "Never thought I'd be out here, homeless in the woods."

"Why are you out here, homeless?" I ask.

Johnny tells us a story about leaving a decent job in Southern Ohio to follow a girl to Akron. The whole thing landed him stranded with a family that's not on speaking terms.

"I won't go back," Johnny says with stubborn certainty. "It ain't so bad out here."

"It's a different story in the winter," Jason says.

"Oh, I won't be here in the winter. I know a guy who's promised me a job in Florida."

We've heard stories like this before, only to see the hoped-for job fall through.

As we walk back to our van, a few students voice how surprised they were with how nice Johnny was.

"What is that a surprise?" Jason asks.

"He just looked so sketchy."

"What made him look sketchy?"

"Well, he had all of those tattoos."

Jason draws the students' attention to his own tattoos. "This make me sketchy?"

"Seriously?" I ask, pointing to the ripped pants my wife won't let me wear in public.

"I'm just surprised, that's all," the student repeats.

"And that's part of the problem," Jason says. "Most people would be surprised, but you're making the effort to learn. That's the difference."

We load back into the van and head toward the High Street Christian Church alley. As we turn from Mill Street into the alley, we see about a dozen people waiting for us. We're expected, and we're late.

"You're late," Stacey informs us as Jason opens his door.

"Nice to see you too, Stacey."

Our students step from the van and go to work, greeting all of their friends, preparing bags of sandwiches and chips and bottled water.

Allen quickly grabs me to show me an article on cats he pulled from the paper. It's about cats bringing their moms and dads dead mice as gifts.

"Did you know they did that?" Allen asks.

"My one cat always keeps the mice for herself," I answer.

"My cat as a kid would always bring me mice, and I'd be like, 'What's this?' Now I know he was bringing me a gift. Isn't that amazing?" Allen's very excited.

"It's messed up," I joke, and the two of us have a laugh.

Allen's a veteran who's waiting for housing, and is very nearly there. He's looking forward to sitting in his apartment and watching *Gunsmoke*.

He begins to show me what movies are playing at the library on Thursday night. As he points out some of the films he wants to see, my attention is stolen by a baby in a stroller. He's being fed pieces of a peanut butter and jelly sandwich on white bread that we have brought. He's a tiny little thing. So innocent and helpless, being raised in an environment that makes him a future statistic. Some students talk in goofy high-pitched voices to him. He smiles. I can't help but think of him in the future, without that smile.

My mind wanders further, and I think of Braiden, a seven-year-old boy we used to visit each week, until his mom overdosed, and he moved away to live with his grandmother. Kids like this stand little chance. Society just waits until these children are older, when these little people grow up desperate and make a mistake—that's when we notice them, when we lock them away.

Some students shout for me, and I'm shaken from the sad images in my head.

"Come see this!"

I give Allen a slap on the back.

"I'll see you next week," Allen says, as I walk away.

"What's up?" I ask the students.

"He can pull his eye out!" a student shouts in my face.

"Huh?"

"I can show you if you want," the man says, in between bites of potato chips.

"Nah, that's alright," I say with a smile.

The kids egg me on, "You afraid?"

"I'll show you," the man says.

"I don't want to put you through the trouble of . . ."

"No," he interrupts, "it comes out easy."

Despite my attempts to keep him from doing it, the man plucks out his prosthetic eyeball and rolls it around in his palm for us to see.

The kids laugh. He laughs. I don't.

"Yep, that's your eyeball," I say, my face probably looking as if I just took a bite of a lemon. "Okay, see you later," I say, walking away.

"I won't," the man says, and my students erupt in laughter.

I step back to take a picture of the alley scene. There's a group of students there, talking with Allen. There's a group handing out bottled water, talking with Bear. There's a couple of kids laughing with Mr. Eyeball, and there's a great scene of one student sitting on the curb talking with a man I've never scene before.

I take the picture. It's one I've taken a dozen times. It captures a moment I love. A moment free of judgment, void of time and place, really. A moment I hope my students remember when they pass the unpopular kids in the hall, and when they're grown and teach their own children about the world. A moment they can take from their back pocket from time to time to bring them back to reality.

THE GHOSTS I RUN WITH

By Matt Tullis

"Creech."

The name escaped my lips somewhere in the third mile of a five-mile run. It was a name I had been trying to think of, off-and-on, for the better part of a decade, the last name of my nurse Janet from Viking Street in Orrville, Ohio.

Janet brought me sausage biscuits from McDonald's just about every morning because it was the only thing I would eat. She was typically my nurse on first shift. She had short brown hair and was about the same age as my mom, and so she felt very motherly to me.

Those things I could remember, but not her last name. Until now.

She died sometime after my initial seventy-day stay at Akron Children's Hospital, which started on January 3, 1991, but I know she must have died during my more than two years of chemotherapy and radiation as an outpatient, time spent eradicating all the leukemic cells in my 15-to-17-year-old body. She died of cancer after years of caring for kids with cancer.

But for a long time, I couldn't remember her last name. I wanted to know her name, her full name, because I felt it was important. I imagined one day reaching out to her family and telling them how much she meant to me when I was near death. And I wouldn't be able to do that if I didn't know her last name, or rather couldn't drag it from the recesses of my brain. It had escaped me for so long, until that run, when I imagined she was just behind me, to the left, running with me, keeping me company as I churned along a black ribbon of asphalt that cuts between two cornfields in northwest Wayne County, Ohio.

There are others. Todd, who lost a leg to osteosarcoma but runs with me nonetheless. He fell off a horse once and his prosthetic leg got caught in the stirrup. Just before he was dragged to death, he reached up and unhooked his fake leg and tumbled down. Then he sat up and laughed like a maniac, like almost being killed by falling off a horse had been the greatest and funniest thing ever to happen in his life.

There's also Melissa. We had the same disease—Acute Lymphoblastic Leukemia—and the same doctor, Dr. Alex Koufos.

She died. I didn't. I think about her a lot when I run. When she runs beside me, I ponder the reasons, if there are any, for the way fate shook out. Our roles very easily could have been reversed, and sometimes I feel like they should have been.

And there's Dr. Koufos himself. He died of bile duct cancer just weeks before I graduated from college (and just after his son, Kosta, who plays for the Memphis Grizzlies, turned nine years old). I've only ever cried at the news of one death, and it was his.

He was the most caring man I've ever known. I think about his raw red hands as they felt my lower abdomen every week on trips to clinic; about the way he would chuckle at my stupid attempts at humor; the way he told me he barely got into college (a lie, but one meant to keep me from freaking out about missing classes in school); and the way he always said my heart sounded strong right after putting the cold stethoscope to my chest. He probably told me my heart was strong maybe a hundred times, and I've long wondered if he meant the organ pumping blood in my chest or something more.

There are more, of course. You can't survive a children's cancer ward and not remember the kids you knew who didn't make it. Terri. Laura Jo. Shelby. Little John. All of them wonderful in their own right and worthy of being remembered forever. All of them ghosts now, wisps of light running beside me mile after mile after mile.

"But this too is true. Stories can save us."

Those are the first two sentences of Tim O'Brien's short story, "The Lives of the Dead," in his book *The Things They Carried*. The story mostly centers around the narrator remembering his nine-year-old self and a girl he loved, Linda, who died of a brain tumor before her tenth birthday. There's a scene in the story when a kid from school tells the narrator that Linda had "kicked the bucket," and at first he didn't understand. It's hard, the first time you've ever been told someone you care about has died. You don't understand and then you think it's a joke and then you refuse to believe, like there's been some cosmic mistake.

Timmy brings Linda back to life by dreaming of her, but the

adult narrator Tim brings her back to life by writing about her. I think about this, too, when I run. I think about Janet's kind brown eyes and Melissa's fearlessness and Todd's craziness and Dr. Koufos's dedication and love and warmth. And then I ask myself, *How have you kept them alive?*

Because that's the bargain in the end, right? That's the answer to the question: *Why did I survive?* Or at least the answer I can live with, one that is better than "no reason at all."

I started running a couple years ago. Until then, I had lived most of my adult life as someone who sat around doing nothing, a lot. Before leukemia, like a lot of kids, I was convinced I would be a professional athlete. After leukemia, I knew that wasn't ever going to happen. Once I got out of high school, where I played baseball and basketball despite undergoing chemotherapy treatments, I stopped competing altogether.

Then one summer, my wife and I took the kids to the beach. When we got back, I saw photos of a man I didn't know, a man who weighed more than 200 pounds. I didn't want to pay for a gym membership, and so instead I bought a cheap pair of shoes at a department store and started going out for a very slow run every morning. My initial goal was to make it to the interstate, which is just over a mile from my house. It took me about two weeks to make it that far without walking. Then I wanted to make it back to my house.

All the while, I had music playing in my ears. I had a little bit of everything stashed on my iPhone—Green Day, Katy Perry, Michael Jackson, the Strokes, even my favorite local band, the Womacks. This included my first half-marathon, which I finished despite leg cramps in both legs at the ten-mile mark. I imagined that the reason I was able to run now, versus the handful of times I had tried earlier in my life and quit, was because of the music, listening to something to distract me from the pain.

Then, after about a year and a half, one day I woke up and went for a run without the music. I don't know why. I just didn't grab my phone before heading out.

I ran four or five miles that morning. It was warm and slightly breezy. I remember running along the mostly flat, straight road that I live on and hearing the wind rustle the tall grasses that lined the ditch. I remember falling into a trance as my feet slapped the pavement and I breathed, *out out in...out out in...*

That's when the ghosts appeared.

Melissa lived in a town just south of where I grew up. I met her at Camp CHOPS, which stands for Hematology and Oncology Patients and Staff, a weekend summer camp. The kids who had cancer got to hang out with the people who took care of them, away from Akron Children's. I went in 1991 as a patient and spent the good portion of that weekend hanging out in the cabin. One night, I listened to the NBA championship, Bulls vs. Lakers, on the radio. While all the other campers were making ice cream sundaes in the dining hall, I was listening to Michael Jordan start construction on his legacy.

In 1992, I was a counselor-in-training, as was Melissa, when we first met. She was a couple years older than me and had an olive complexion and tight, short curly hair, the kind that was starting to grow back, to reclaim space it had once held but lost. She was cute, and because of that, and because I desperately needed someone who knew exactly what I had gone through in the last year-and-a-half, I instantly developed a crush on her.

We all hung out with some other kids, including Ben, who was the son of my clinic nurse, Pam, and Kim and Sharon, both teenagers who had long ago defeated their childhood cancers.

Melissa and I were still in the thick of it, though. We still battled baldness and the inability to walk without tripping, our feet unable to navigate even the smallest contours in a sidewalk because they had been deadened by massive doses of Vincristine. We still vomited our brains out after getting chemo and missed extensive amounts of school.

We hung out a handful of times outside of Camp CHOPS too. We talked on the phone occasionally. I don't know what we talked about, although I suspect it was probably regular teenage stuff.

There was nothing worse, we felt, than being considered "not normal." We wanted to be normal more than anything in the world. We wanted to be teenagers, not teenagers with leukemia.

We got "better." She went off to college and then so did I. We didn't stay in touch after that. Why? I don't know. I had her phone number pinned on my bulletin board, and it went with me to college, but I never picked up the phone, partly because she was a part of my past, the past I was trying to shed now that I was in a place where nobody knew about my illness.

Once I got to college, I was normal again, and I suspect she felt the same way. She didn't call, either. I think calling one another would acknowledge that we were not, indeed, normal. We were different. We were still teenagers with leukemia. We would always be the kid walking like a stork, picking our knees up high so our dead feet wouldn't stumble. We would always be the teenager who is bald, the kid who is skinny, the child who knew and was not afraid of death. We would always be teenagers with leukemia.

Then I went home one weekend and picked up the newspaper and saw her obituary.

There's another reason I started running, beyond hoping to lose weight, which I did, forty pounds in less than six months. That was because I would like to live long enough to see my two kids—my ten-year-old son Emery and my seven-year-old daughter Lily—become adults.

Childhood cancer survivors are twice as likely to develop a secondary cancer in their lifetime, primarily because most of the drugs and treatments used in the 1990s to treat childhood cancer were themselves carcinogenic. And if they don't cause cancer, they often make the heart, the bones, the lungs, and just about every other part of the body weaker and more prone to later-in-life health issues.

Through my 20s and even into my 30s, I didn't really care about any of that. Partly it was because I didn't know about that stuff. But having kids of my own made me greedy. I survived having leukemia when I was fifteen, and now, more than twenty years later, I was struck with a worry—who knows if it was rational or not—that I was going to die a young death, and I wanted more time than that. I figured the best way to make that happen was to get in shape.

And so I ran. In 2013, I ran 617 miles. In 2014, I ran another 672 miles. I want to run 1,000 in a year, and then after that, I want to run 2,000. Even now, as I sit here in the best shape of my life, able to slip on a pair of running shoes and head out the door and knock off eight miles without even thinking about it, I still worry about dying young. I don't fear it, but I don't like the fact that it is possible. I've long felt that I'm living on borrowed time.

I started writing about being sick almost immediately after I stopped being sick. Or rather, once I had finished my treatments. The first thing I wrote about having leukemia was for a scholarship contest with *Guideposts Magazine*. It was a religious publication, so I sprinkled a lot of "Praise Gods" and "I really think I'm a miracle." I didn't win.

In college, I kept leukemia to myself for the most part, not wanting it to color people's perception of me. But I wrote about it a lot. Then, in my final semester as an undergraduate student, I took a creative writing workshop. I wrote about it in that class, and I kept writing about it on the side. In grad school, I wrote a memoir about having leukemia. In my various jobs as a reporter, I've always found ways to write about kids with cancer or myself with cancer. I just can't seem to not write about it.

I've thought long and hard about why it keeps circling back to that time in my life that I had leukemia, and I never had an answer. Part of it, I realize now that I'm older, stems from the fact that I've been trying to make sense of what happened. Sufferers of trauma do that. They weave what happened to them into a narrative that allows them to see a larger meaning.

I've just never been able to see what that larger meaning was. At least I wasn't able to until I started running and my ghosts started running with me. I've been writing about that time in my life to keep Melissa and Dr. Koufos and Janet and everyone else alive. To let them live forever in words, a place that cancer can't touch.

We had a support group at Akron Children's Hospital for kids with cancer that met, I think, on Wednesday nights. There were some longer-term survivors, late teens who were no longer in danger of relapsing, in the group. And then there were those of us who were currently undergoing treatment. It was something I looked forward to more than anything else in my life, which at that point consisted mostly of sitting in my bed at home and numbing myself each day by watching the same old reruns on television: *I Love Lucy, The Beverly Hillbillies, Gilligan's Island.*

The meetings often coincided with a trip to the clinic for me to receive my outpatient chemotherapy. After spending two or three hours in the treatment room, having dangerous chemicals pumped into my body, Mom and I would head over to the Ronald McDonald House and watch TV until later in the evening. Then I would head back to the hospital, somewhere on the fourth floor, where the support group met, close to where I had lived for seventy days in the winter and spring of 1991.

The group was led by a social worker named Nancy. She was the first person I met at Akron Children's the day I arrived there. Kind and soft-spoken, she had a round face and soft blond hair. She laughed—or maybe chuckled is a better word—at everything that wasn't specifically related to our illnesses. Her laugh was always quiet, but it was real and something that was sorely needed on a childhood cancer ward. She spent a lot of time in my room, talking to me, talking to my parents, making sure we knew that if we ever needed anything, anything, we simply had to ask.

I don't remember specifically what we talked about in that support group. I don't remember how many times we met, although I do remember thinking it wasn't often enough. I remember eating snacks. I remember going to a lab and having the technicians show us how they do blood tests. I remember one of the girls, Shelby or maybe Laura Jo, talking about going to prom. I remember sitting next to Curt, who loved basketball, and across from Tim, who was a swimmer. I remember Terri being wheeled into the room in her hospital bed. I remember feeling at home with these people. My tribe of sick kids.

Earlier, before we were a support group, Tim, the swimmer, came up with an idea for a board game for kids with cancer. He called it "Road to Remission." The players drew cards, and then moved plastic game pieces around a board, either forward or backward, depending on what the card said. When I was still a resident of the fourth floor at Akron Children's, Nancy brought in a stack of index cards and a marker and asked me to write stuff down on the cards. She told me to write about good things that happen to you when you're in the hospital, battling cancer as a kid, and the bad things. And then she told me to assign each of them a number of spaces to move forward or backward.

I imagine I wrote mostly bad things down. I had a rough time in the hospital. I developed an infection, probably bacterial meningitis, on my brain, which is what kept me in there for so long. I became severely depressed because it didn't seem like I was ever going to go home. I had gotten to the point where I was fine with death, to where I didn't fear it anymore. I probably wrote about feeding tubes getting clogged and physical therapists making you walk down the hallway and nurses waking you up in the middle of the night.

There were good things, though. Nurses like Janet who brought me sausage biscuits and doctors like Dr. Koufos who really, truly cared. There was another nurse, John, who gave me a Ricky Henderson rookie card. I hope I wrote that stuff down, too.

Obviously, there were enough good things written down so that players could actually make it to remission. It wasn't the kind of game you could ever lose. The point was to get everyone to talk about their experiences. But sometimes I wonder if we wrote too many good things down, if maybe not every player should have made it to remission, at least not if we wanted it to be a realistic portrayal of the lives of the game's creators.

The hospital turned it into a full-fledged board game. We even shot a commercial. *Good Morning America* heard about the game and did a segment on it. Tim flew to New York City to talk about it with host Joan Lunden. Then Lunden read the names of the other creators and showed our photos, including mine.

But then, the caveat—five of the eight creators had died. Only Tim, Michael, and myself reached remission. And then, not really.

Many, many years later, I was thinking about Tim. Probably after a run. I called Pam, the nurse who called to tell me Dr. Koufos had died, and the one person at Akron Children's I have managed to stay in touch with. I asked her where Tim was and what he was doing.

"Oh, Matt," she said.

He had been a ghost for quite some time.

I ran my first marathon, the Akron Marathon, in September 2014, raising funds for the Leukemia and Lymphoma Society's Team-in-Training and collected more than $1,500 for blood cancer research. And I chose Akron because the race finishes in the shadow of Akron Children's Hospital. The finish line is home plate in Canal Park, home of the Akron RubberDucks, a Double-A minor league baseball team. As you make your way into the stadium, if you look up and to the right, you see the blue-and-white logo of Akron Children's, perched up on a parking garage that overlooks the baseball stadium, by a footbridge to the place I called home so long ago.

Around mile twenty, as we ran through a gorgeous tree-lined neighborhood, we came upon a water stop. I was starting to slow. My friend Stuart and I had been keeping about a 9:45-minute pace throughout the race, but my brain was starting to go. I had only run twenty miles once before, three weeks earlier. I was hitting a wall.

I walked up to the water stop and reached out for a cup. I recognized her face immediately, one that hadn't changed a bit since the first day I met her nearly 24 years earlier.

"Nancy!" I shouted.

"That's me," she said.

I don't think she recognized me, and in my 20th-mile stupor, I never told her who I was. I imagine it probably dawned on her later. But the recognition for me was immediate, and so I hugged her and probably freaked her out. And then I moved on, energized, feeling once more that everything would be all right, that I would make it to the finish line.

My energy lasted about three more miles. That's when my legs cramped. Three miles from the finish, again. I told Stuart to go on. He had been battling an Achilles issue and slowing down made his foot and leg hurt even worse.

I started walking and stretched. I got going again, and then, toward the end, was coming down South Main Street, toward Canal Park. I looked off to the right and saw the hospital. My room and the place our support group met had long since been demolished and replaced with a big, new, fancy hospital floor, but I could see where my hospital room had once been, where I had once looked out a window from my hospital bed onto the streets of Akron, streets I was now running. I thought about those days and nights when my mom or dad begged me to get out of bed, to take a walk down the hallway, just to sit up, to care, to want to live. I thought about the nights I couldn't sleep, and the nights I could. I thought about the day I was supposed to have brain surgery to remove that infection, and how that surgery was called off at the last minute. I thought about how, when I got out of the hospital, I couldn't walk from my bedroom to the kitchen without getting exhausted, without feeling dead.

As my feet shuffled along the road, I thought of Melissa and how we used to walk like storks. I thought about Dr. Koufos and all the times he told me my heart was strong, and how, on this day, it had powered me through more than 25 miles, how it had just a little bit more work to do, and I realized that it really was strong, both physically and metaphorically. And I thought about how I missed him a great deal. I missed all of them so, so much. I imagined they were all with me, some of them lining the streets with the other spectators who were screaming and yelling and holding up signs. And others, like Melissa and Dr. Koufos, were running at my side, with me every step.

My feet plodded on, along the Akron pavement. The hospital disappeared behind other tall buildings in downtown and then I made a turn and then another turn and I was in the stadium.

I didn't look up at the hospital. I looked forward, toward the finish line. I ran as hard as I could, and I crossed it almost sprinting.

I walked through the chute and turned right and then I saw it. The hospital. I took a few more steps, but then I had to stop and sit down. I needed to look at the hospital and think. I was exhausted and needed to just stop after more than four hours and 44 minutes of forward movement.

I used to joke after a run that I felt like I was dead, but I've stopped making that joke because it is ridiculous. Every time I finish any run, no matter how exhausted I might be, I feel more alive than I ever have in my life.

I remember one recurring dream I had during my seventy days as a resident of Akron Children's. I remember it because of how alive it made me feel, how strong and powerful, at a time when I couldn't even get out of bed to take a bath. In the dream, I am running down a hill behind my old elementary school. I'm carrying a baseball glove and a ball, and I'm running, fast.

I used to see this dream as one about baseball, because of the glove and ball, and because baseball was my sport. But in the dream I never actually got to a field to play ball. I just kept running.

I've reframed that dream as one about running now, and I think about that dream whenever I run now, remembering how I wished I could just keep going, forever. And I think about my ghosts, and think if I keep running and writing forever, I can keep them alive. They can stay right here beside me, mile after mile after mile, word by word.

FOR NEW REFUGEES, AKRON IS MORE THAN A PLACE, IT'S A HOME

By Maria Mancinelli

Akron's North Hill has long been an immigrant neighborhood—its demographic history visible through markets, pizza shops, and community centers established over the years by the Italians, Polish, and Irish. But recently the neighborhood has seen an influx of refugees from Southeast Asia.

I first became aware of these new groups of refugees when I returned to Akron in early 2013 after being away for seven years. I had just spent a year in Brazil and planned to return as soon as I could figure out my visa and job situation. The idea of spending more than a couple months in my hometown was completely incomprehensible at the time. As I applied for jobs in Brazil and in major cities in the U.S., a friend suggested I inquire about job openings at the International Institute of Akron (IIA). I was vaguely familiar with IIA and its work with immigrants, as it was just a five-minute drive from my parents' home in Cuyahoga Falls. I was not interested in a job that committed me to stay in Akron, but called to see if there were any internship opportunities. By the following week I had committed to a three-month internship, and after those three months I accepted a long-term position.

The International Institute of Akron, located in an unassuming brick building on Tallmadge Avenue in North Hill, is a leading refugee resettlement agency in Northeast Ohio, welcoming and helping hundreds of people to make their new home in Akron each year. Its work with both immigrants and refugees has impacted the makeup of Akron as a whole, but is particularly visible in North Hill, where incoming refugees rent homes and apartments with the assistance of IIA, and have independently opened businesses. The evident multicultural influences brought by the newest refugees to North Hill supplements its rich immigrant history and original neighborhood framework.

Though I grew up near Akron, my memories of North Hill are few: driving down North Main Street to reach downtown, buying cake from Crest Bakery, and eating at Swensons. Until I began interning with IIA, I was unaware of the great presence of refugees in Akron, and even that the United States had a Refugee Admissions Program. I can remember from a very young age wanting to leave the Akron area, a place I believed offered a low quality of life in respect to the world at large. I never considered it a place to start and advance my career. And my regard for Akron upon returning was about the same as when I had left at eighteen.

What I did find in Akron in 2013 was a lot of people working to attract and retain millennials, to highlight Akron's good and bad, and to improve the city and unite its communities. I did not remember a city so aware of its complexities, yet so hopeful about its potential. It seemed that Akron was looking for people to declare their love for it and commit to making it better. After nearly three years of working with the refugee communities in North Hill, I realized that Akron was not just a place people chose randomly for resettlement in the United States, it was their home, a place for a new start and chance in life, a place of opportunity, for themselves and their children, a place to learn, share, and appreciate, a place to make better, and to love.

There are millions of refugees in the world and less than one percent will ever have the chance to resettle in a city like Akron. The United States has the largest resettlement program in the world, taking about 70,000 refugees each year, of which, annually more than 500 have been coming directly to Akron in recent years. Resettlement is not easy and integration is contingent upon the city's available resources and willingness to welcome refugees. My newfound appreciation of Akron developed as I recognized that my hometown was welcoming and giving refuge to so many who were profoundly grateful to claim the city as their home.

I was fortunate to meet and befriend many refugees while in Akron. There is one family with whom I became particularly close, who gave me much insight on the refugee resettlement experience, and for whose friendship I will be forever grateful. My first year in Akron I taught English classes twice a week in the evening. After I stopped teaching, I kept in contact with a few of my students and was invited to one former student's party to celebrate the birth of her daughter. She lives in North Hill and as I approached her home it was apparent it was a large gathering by the dozens of shoes tossed about her front porch. I was offered a noodle soup as soon as

I entered, and two young girls willingly brought it to me. They introduced themselves as the host's nieces, speaking without accents and handling themselves as any teenager would. I was impressed by how quickly and effortlessly they could switch between Burmese and English. We chatted, played with their two younger siblings and many cousins, and made plans to do something one upcoming weekend.

Within weeks I had met the two girls' entire family—their mom, dad, older brother and sister, sister's husband and baby, and younger brother and sister. They were eight in total and their rented home on North Hill was a revolving door of friends and family coming to talk, celebrate, play, and eat. They had resettled in Akron in 2008, after spending more than a decade in a refugee camp in Thailand, now joined by several other friends and family. They spoke Burmese at home and switched between it and English when hosting non-Burmese-speaking guests and when about town. The parents dressed in traditional garments, while their children wore American clothing with hints of Asian influences. They ate Burmese food, shopping at the Asian stores in Akron and Cleveland, although the older brother admitted to regularly eating fish sandwiches from McDonald's. Some of them worked, some attended school, and some cared for the home.

I began to stop by regularly after work to catch up with the family and occasionally eat with them. They would always offer me Burmese coffee and, as is the custom, would not let me help clean up or even take my glass or plate into the kitchen. Witnessing their hospitality has changed how I receive guests and friends in my own home. I always called or wrote before I went over, asking if they would be home and if I could stop by, and they always replied in some version of "of course, you do not have to ask." I liked the spontaneity of getting together with them and the easygoing atmosphere they created.

In 2015, several residents presented to Akron City Council a resolution to designate Akron a "Welcoming City," as part of the national Welcoming America initiative. One of the daughters agreed to speak about her family's experience. She told Akron's councilmen:

My parents came to the United States so their kids could get a better education and have a better life. In Thailand it is hard to get a good education. My parents want my brothers and sisters and me to be successful, they want us to go to college and they support me in my dream of becoming a nurse.

I think it is important for Akron to welcome immigrants and refugees because they come with many ideas and different perspectives. I see what my own family offers to the community: we are driven, motivated, we work hard; strive to get a good education and we want to give back to this community.

Akron is my home. I love Akron and want to make it a more welcoming place for everyone.

The resolution passed that evening.

It is not uncommon to hear talk around Akron about the benefits of welcoming refugees to the city and the economic advantages from which North Hill has especially profited. Homes are being bought, maintained, and fixed up; businesses open so quickly that we could not keep up with updating the neighborhood asset map. It was rumored that North High School would have closed if not for the hundreds of refugee students who now fill its hallways, and you find people, a lot of people, outside, working in their gardens, walking to the local market, picking their children up from school. North Hill is vibrant and I cannot help but marvel at how quickly the refugees who come directly to Akron, as well as those who come from other cities and states in the U.S., have dedicated themselves to this city.

In her presentation to Akron City Council, my friends' daughter was clear about her intention to stay in Akron, saying:

After I graduate high school I want to go to the University of Akron to study nursing.

After I graduate from college I want to get a job and work in Akron.

She, like so many others who arrived in Akron as refugees, is committed to Akron and to making a good life here. Their impact is evident through the changing landscape of North Hill and beyond. And when talking about that impact, I almost always find myself beginning with economic benefits, offsetting population loss, or the desire by millennials to live in a multicultural city. Although all are notable, where I have found the most important and impactful benefits of having refugees in Akron, is in the friendships I have with them. It is through these personal connections that I have come to love and appreciate this city. Through graduations and Sunday dinners, to celebrating first Ramadans and Thanksgivings, we have shared, questioned, and admired each other's culture and traditions. My relationship with this family has brought me closer to my own and given me immeasurable insight on life.

Akron has opened its doors wide to many of the world's most vulnerable. I can imagine that refugees appreciate Akron's low cost of living, beautiful parks, and job availabilities, but I believe what keeps them in Akron, and keeps them thriving here, are the people who welcomed them with open arms, who smile when they pass them on the sidewalk, who coach their child's soccer team, who are patient when they sign up for a bank account or library card, and who befriend them. My hope is that Akronites continue to open themselves to such friendships to fully understand and appreciate our new neighbors' impact on the community.

COOL BUT NOT TOO COOL: THE ALLURE OF AKRON

By Roza Maille

It seems like a mystery to outsiders why people stay here. I ponder this myself, reflecting on the journey that brought me to my home in Akron. I grew up in a rural area of Northeast Ohio and as a youngster, like many, I couldn't wait to live somewhere adventurous and more importantly, far away. I would dream about big cities and all the possibilities they would hold, all the great things I could accomplish if only I could leave. Of course there is a lure about the rocky west coast, the bright lights of New York City, and the beauty of southern France, but you can never really get that Ohio dirt out from under your fingernails.

Did my developing adolescent brain ever think I would live here in Akron for more than a decade? Honestly, I probably didn't even know where Akron was back then. I had a friend move here when I was in first grade and it might as well have been Los Angeles, since I rarely traveled beyond the nearby towns of Salem or Alliance, except for an occasional shopping trip. The buildings here are way taller than where I grew up, so I guess that's a start. What about all those perceived big city opportunities I was missing out on? The great things I was to accomplish? It's true that Akron is a little rugged around the edges, but let me see if I can describe the charm of Rust Belt Ohio and the grittiness that fosters creativity.

I first lived outside Northeast Ohio when I went to Belgium for a year as a foreign exchange student. Before I left, basically the only thing I knew about the country was that it bordered France and they have good waffles and chocolate there. Both are very true. But despite its European *je ne sais quoi*, at its core Belgium was a lot like Ohio; gloomy, underrated, and nobody really wanted to vacation there—which was comforting in a way. But Belgium, like Ohio, is in the center of so many great things and places. After living abroad, I crashed with my best friend in New York City briefly, moving in, with impeccable timing, at the end of August 2001. Witnessing 9/11 and its bleak and chaotic aftermath was somewhat overwhelming, as you can imagine, and "far away" suddenly didn't seem so appealing to me anymore.

I spent my late teens and early twenties in Kent, just one county over from Akron. I moved there to attend Kent State University and study art. Originally, I planned to go to an art school in Philadelphia, but those plans fell through. Kent was a safe bet, since I had already had a bad experience living out of state and most of my friends lived there.

Our band of misfits found comfort and support in one another. We would spend most of our days sleepily stumbling to our classes, and our nights drinking Black Label at a local hole-in-the-wall punk club called the Mantis. Bands like Kill the Hippies, Lester, Don Austin, Dexter Chumley Attack, and Crimson Sweet would draw in mosh pits of teenagers, all converging to drink, smoke, and beat the hell out of each other. The BYOB policy was appealing to underage drinkers. The regulars all knew the cover charge was really how much you told Sam (the owner) you had in your pocket. Most just handed over a crumpled dollar or two and he would begrudgingly stamp Yosemite Sam from Looney Tunes on the back of your hand in purple ink.

As you can see, everything was very legit and official. I never once stepped foot in the bathroom because I was convinced I would catch some mutated form of hepatitis, based on how those who ventured in described it. The dim lights in the rest of the place could conceal a lot; I'm sure there were disgusting things lurking on the floors. I remember cringing when an out-of-town band's singer performed in her bare feet, not to mention a random drunk dude who thought getting naked and falling on the stage would be a brilliant idea. The Mantis (R.I.P.) was eventually shut down for fire code violations soon after the infamous fatal fire at a Great White concert in a Rhode Island night club in 2003.

During this time we all heard about how Devo, whose members were from Kent and Akron, played over at Fat Jimmy's, which was called JB's Down Under back in the day (members of the band also attended art school at KSU). The old JB's hosted a variety of punk and rock acts before they made it big. The venue, which would later be named JB's once again, was actually right across the street from the Mantis. At school, I was impressed with stories about how Chrissie Hynde, the Akron native of Pretenders fame, once took a printmaking class there. The professor claimed to have a print of hers back in a flat file somewhere. I didn't know it yet, but Akron was seeping into my psyche.

All these stories made us long for those cooler, punker days –but they also inspired us to build on the already existing outsider subculture. We eventually realized that growing up in this area actually nurtured creativity. Creativity came to us in the form of no-budget horror movies, experimental noise bands, tattoos, handmade Halloween costumes, a bicycle gang called the "Psycho Riders," and general shenanigans usually involving cheap beer and house shows. We would stay up late talking about music, movies, our imminent futures after college, our disdain for frat boys, our collective creative endeavors, and our theories about the character-building properties of the Midwest.

I even ran into a friend from first grade who'd moved away to Akron years before, at a house show, at a place behind the Mantis called the Taint. She claimed she recognized me because of my hair. This was somewhat concerning considering I had a home haircut that resembled an '80s hair-metal style at the time. This makes me wonder...had Akron been seeping into my subconscious all these years, even when I lived in Kent? It's like the twist at the end of a movie. You don't really see all the clues the filmmaker revealed to you until you watch it a second time (*à la* "I see dead people"). There are so many TV shows and movies that name-drop Akron as a general "small town, middle of nowhere" city. It's partially because of this that I find Akron so interesting. It's small enough to be largely unknown but mentioned enough in pop culture to suggest there must be some allure behind its rough façade.

During the waning of my college years, cheap rent drew me to Akron. The neighboring city had sort of tall, sometimes abandoned buildings, and a music club called the Lime Spider that hosted a great variety of local and national rock and punk/experimental bands (it closed its doors in 2007, but is now one of my favorite Akron restaurants, the Lockview). Akron looked cool—not only was there urban decay, which I love, but it had Art Deco architecture downtown and Tudor-style homes in its neighborhoods. Old-style neon signs still shone at night at places like Swensons Drive-In (home of the famous Galley Boy hamburger) and the Mary Coyle's ice cream shop. Flashy marquees were lit up at the Highland Square movie theater and the historic Akron Civic Theatre. It was intriguing and a little scary, just like those teenage mosh pits at the Mantis. It felt like something could go horribly wrong, but it was still worth going in headfirst just to see what it was like.

I moved to Akron in search of cheaper rent; I stayed because I could see the potential in this city that I now call home. I won't lie, it took a few years; the revelation was fairly recent. But as an artist and arts administrator, I can see things changing for the better. An energy is bubbling in the arts community as more creatives are choosing to stay instead of moving to a "cool" city.

I've heard people say many times, "Akron is a great place...to grow up." This is of course followed by a chuckle and a snide comment about the crappy weather. I will counter that by saying that for me and for others, Akron has been a great place to grow. Through my experiences at community galleries, and by getting to know leaders in different neighborhoods through my job at the Akron Art Museum, I have found many motivated and creative Akronites who will work hard to make things happen for their community. We have our own indie craft fair, Crafty Mart, that continues to grow, a new indie movie theater called the Nightlight, street festivals like Porch Rokr, where bands play on neighborhood porches, and a monthly paper called the Devilstrip where you can read all about the other great things happening in our city. All of these things, plus many more I'm not mentioning, were started by the aforementioned motivated and creative Akronites who are not only people who grew up here but people who moved here later in life like me.

What I like about Akron is that it is cool, but not too cool. We are cool enough to have street festivals all summer long, but not cool enough to have a disruptively huge music festival like South by Southwest that all the locals loathe. We are cool enough to attract young professionals and artists, but not cool enough to entice detrimental gentrification complete with skyrocketing rent prices. We are cool enough to spawn people like artist/musician Mark Mothersbaugh, indie filmmaker Jim Jarmusch, internationally known comics artist/graphic novelist Derf Backderf, Grammy-award winning band the Black Keys, poet laureate Rita Dove, and bands and musicians like the Waitresses, Tin Huey, Rachel Sweet, and Tim "Ripper" Owens. And we can't forget about basketball legend LeBron James.

Some of the negative things you've probably heard about this city are true. Akron needs real improvements—crime, abandoned property, and poverty are all problems. You can hear crickets in our downtown on the weekends. But despite the remnants of its industrial downfall, I believe Akron can be saved by its people. Innovation is what got the city here in the first place, and I believe those roots are still grounded here. Behind any great art is a struggle, and a story that needs to be told. If there's anything that Akron has in its favor, it's a good story.

WEEK 13

THE DOORMAN
DIARIES

By Jeff Shearl

I: The Bringer of Light

When the office phone rang Gavin sighed. The caller ID read STEW-ART, THOMAS. Gavin paused the Jack Johnson music video he had been watching over and over again and picked up the receiver.

"Doormen's office," he said. It was barely an office, being only about big enough for the computer desk and the mini-fridge that housed rotting lunches and a few old ketchup packets.

"Ok, we will," he said and hung up.

He turned to me. "Looks like you're learning lights today."

Downstairs, behind a black door, was a room divided in half by a chain link gate. On one side were some old vacuums and a bunch of Kleenex boxes. On the other was the most expensive room within the University of Akron's E.J. Thomas Performing Arts Hall. Simply referred to as "The Light Bulb Room," it contained back-up bulbs for every single light in the building. Thousands of dollars of fragile glass rested on thick, floor-to-ceiling shelves.

Gavin showed me where the useful lights were. He was only a little taller than me, about 5' 7", so he made use of the stepladder in most cases. He pulled a small box from the shelf, opened it, and unwrapped a spiral of foam padding, revealing a light bulb about the size of my pinky. The glass was cloudy. He held it carefully by the base in front of his pale blue eyes.

"These are called halogens," he said. "We have to wear oven gloves to change them, or else they'll burn you when you put them in, and if the oil from your hand gets on them they explode."

"Why use them?" I asked.

"This place is fucked, that's why."

After grabbing a box of halogens, Gavin pointed out a swollen tampon adhered to the ceiling. According to Gavin tampons will stick to cement when they get wet, and according to doorman legend, this particular tampon has been on the ceiling since the early 90's.

We had to push the bucket lift around the outside of the building because there was no other way from backstage, where the lift was kept, to the lobby that didn't involve stairs. The lift was silver and had a shaky bucket about two feet by two feet square. The sidewalk was bumpy, partly because it was old, and partly because someone had planted trees in it and the roots were prying up the cement. E.J. itself was pure concrete with floor-to-ceiling windows ascending the several stories. The ceiling sloped, which made the placements of the light fixtures slope as well. Some of them were only ten feet from the ground, while others were more than fifty feet above the busy modern carpet.

It was my first time in a lift, and I'll admit I was nervous. Not because of the height, but because of the volatile bomb I was shoving into an electrical socket. My first light was one of the highest in the building. Gavin had me do this one because he believed it would eliminate any apprehension I held about heights. I think he was afraid of heights.

The spaces for the light fixtures often curved inside the ceiling, so it wasn't a straight shot from where your hand entered the fixture to the actual socket. I had to contort my body into weird shapes while struggling with the bulkiness of the furnace glove. Then it was a matter of angling the bulb the right way and popping it in. They didn't screw, they just kind of twisted in. Because of this design, I have seen these bulbs turn on, get hot, then promptly fall from the socket, becoming a modern Greek fire when hitting the ground, sending hot glass flying in all directions. Several times during this day I got the glove stuck in the socket after the light came on. In about two seconds the oven glove would be burnt through to my hand. The smell was almost as bad as the implication. Think burnt hair, but with a chemical component.

When Gavin and I had about finished, one of our managers, Tom, came meandering toward us. He was tall and walked with a limp. Not a gaudy limp that says, "I've lived dangerously," but a normal, dignified limp that says, "I have arthritis." His gray hair was abandoning ship from the middle of his head. He told us the lobby looked good, and that we could return to our office after we made sure the stairways were finished. Doormen were supposed to stay in the office to guard the stage door from any trespassers, but most of the time we just watched Netflix or played Halo on the secret Xbox on our "broken" television.

As we climbed the stairs, Gavin was quiet. His face was stuck in an apprehensive frown. The staircase started out with low ceilings, with the light fixtures hanging on the bottom of the landing above. I could almost reach a few of them. Much to my relief these fixtures didn't have halogen bulbs, they had a larger variation of a standard light bulb. However, as we started getting higher the lights did too, and at the top I saw why Gavin seemed so upset.

There was one burnt-out light positioned almost directly above the stairs, and it was high, about forty feet. I asked Gavin how we'd change it, because we couldn't get the lift up there. He said, "The Giant." I thought he was making a joke. We went to a storage closet, and in it was a ladder with "LITTLE GIANT" printed on the side. It had telescoping legs, and it was the only ladder big enough that started out small enough to fit where we needed it. It was heavy, and once we got it set up it was obviously not tall enough for us to stand on and reach. I was led to another storage closet. This time Gavin got a long yellow pole. There was suction cup with a string threaded through it on the end. The idea was the light stuck in the suction cup, and once you were pretty sure it was in the fixture enough you would yank the string, releasing the bulb from the cup.

We were finally set up to change the bulb. We extended the ladder so the front legs were on the landing, and the back were on the second step down. Gavin began to scale it. He made it up three rungs and tried from there. The pole, even at its longest length, came nowhere near the fixture. Gavin was shaking a little, and admitted that being on the ladder so near the stairs was making him nervous. It made me nervous too, but I tried. I climbed the ladder high enough to reach.

It was dizzying to stand so high and look straight up. I felt like I wasn't attached to anything, that I should be falling. My vision shook, my heart beat heavy, and I started to feel hot. When the suction cup made contact with the burnt bulb it didn't stick. Instead it pushed the fixture up. Gavin had failed to mention that the fixtures were held to the ceiling by some kind of rope, so they would swing around. I became aware of my shins touching the step above the one on which I stood. It was like my body wanted me to be aware of what I would be missing out on if I fell.

I got angry, and just jabbed the pole into the socket, and it stuck. This eased my mind, and before I knew it I had the bulb out, and Gavin was handing me the replacement. While I raised the new bulb to its position I pictured it falling toward me from up there. Would I anticipate it and leap from the ladder myself, or would I freeze up, be hit with it, then fall? I had to battle with the fixture to stop the swinging, and the bulb found its place. I turned it, and the light started to flicker on. It was still flickering when it wouldn't turn anymore, and after I had pulled the string to release the suction, and after we had taken the ladder down. While we were collapsing the light pole, the bulb burnt out, and little wisps of smoke unfurled from all parts of it.

"Ballast must have burnt out," Gavin said. "We can't change that one."

II: Bird Graveyard

The caller ID read FELDER, CARRIE.

"Doormen's office," I said.

"Yeah um," Carrie said, "there's a bird in the lobby."

"We'll take care of it."

I hung up and turned to Donald. He was a bigger guy with glasses and short brown hair.

"Bird in the lobby," I said.

"OK, Jeffrey," he said, hiking his jeans up as he stood. "Let's see what we can do."

If Health & Safety were to find a dead bird in the building the night of a show, we could be in a lot of trouble: inspections, maybe even a meeting. So this was of the utmost importance. A bird flies into the building about once a year, and Donald has been there every time. He told me they usually die because they try to fly out the closed windows and get brain damage. It's a sad way to go, and Donald has always tried to chase the birds out.

We found the bird perched in plastic bamboo that accents the large doors to the green room. It wasn't too far away from an outside door, which we opened. We tried to shoo the bird outside by making loud noises and chasing it in that direction. The bird succeeded in flying everywhere but out the door, and eventually abandoned the bamboo in favor of hiding under the info desk. It was chirping.

"Don't we have nets somewhere?" I asked Donald.

"Don't think so," he said.

"We should check the Shelf of Random Ass Things," I said.

"I love the Shelf of Random Ass Things," Donald said.

Everyone loves the Shelf of Random Ass Things.

The Shelf of Random Ass Things was a massive shelf in the paint pit. The paint pit itself held several oddities that had no other home in the building, including four charcoal grills, a walker, and an old washing machine, but these pale in comparison to the Shelf of Random Ass Things. The shelf had nothing of real use on it. Boxes of plastic bowler hats, rubber masks of U.S. presidents, a large container of neon green wrist bands with something written on them in Spanish, attachable toilet-seat armrests, boxes of checker boards, and more. We figured the Shelf of Random Ass Things might have a net, but it didn't.

But it did have dowel rods. We took four of the thin wooden rods upstairs. There was some plastic sheeting in the tool room usually used for covering the carpet in makeshift catering kitchens we set up in the lobby for receptions. We cut a square of sheeting and taped it to the dowel rods. Behold! The latest in doorman ingenuity! A bird net!

Filled with confidence, Donald and I returned to the lobby, each with our own net, but found no bird. We found it in one of the bathrooms, dead on the floor.

"What do we do with it, Donald?" I asked.

"Well Jeffrey," he said, "it seems wrong to throw it away, right?"

"Right."

"I'll show you where we put them."

Donald scooped the fragile brown carcass into his net. I followed him outside. There was a large concrete plaza attached to E.J. Thomas. It had a few picnic tables that were always unoccupied because of the blinding sun. Donald and I staggered through the waving heat toward a shady corner. Decorative bushes lined the border, blocking the train tracks below. Donald went to the farthest bushes and let the bird slide from his net. It got caught in the leaves. We prodded it until it reached the dusty bottom of the planter. We stood on that hallowed ground for a few moments before going back inside.

III: Nemesis

The phone display read EJ LOBBY. On the other end of the line was an usher. He told me to call UAPD and come out. When my old dress shoes, with their peeling vinyl and salt stains, touched the busy red carpet of the lobby, I was greeted by frenzied crafters. Mostly women, mostly middle-aged, mostly suburban. They were here to sell expensive, hand-crafted signs and apple butter at our annual craft show. They weren't prepared for the city to seep in. To get this close. This real. It was my job to keep the city out, and somehow it got in.

"Where is he?" I asked at the info desk, trying to keep cool.

"Robertson Lobby, but now we can't find him."

"Can't find him?"

"He was in Robertson –"

"Never mind, just wait for the police."

I went to Robertson, and sure enough there was no sign of the homeless man who had somehow wandered in despite the locked doors, laid in the middle of the floor, and started screaming. I couldn't believe that anyone would let him out of their sight after that, much less that everyone would. I asked a few crafters. No one saw where he went.

Once the police arrived, we did a building walk-through. There were places he could have gone where no one would find him for months. We never found him, so we assumed he just wandered out in the commotion. The officers got a description from the usher at the front desk: a shorter guy with dirty red hair. Looked like it had not been uncut for too long. He had wire-frame glasses that were all taped together, and really baggy clothes. The usher told the officers the man was drunk and asked to use the restroom.

The next day I worked I relieved a doorman named Ian. When I walked in he was wearing his socks and looking mighty unhappy about it. When I asked him why, he told me that he had stepped in human poop that had been excreted near the back door, and placed with such care that it was impossible to have seen it before stepping in it. He was the first in a long line of doormen to find maliciously placed fecal matter. Each time our cleaning staff reported seeing a man fitting the description of the craft show screamer, we found poop outside that door the next day. The doormen began calling him the "Door Shitter," a nickname I thought to be insensitive at first, but found difficult to abandon for its accurate description of the state of things.

I didn't see him in person until summer. We were moving furniture near the windows, and he walked right up to the glass. His eyes were deeply bagged and dark. His sweaty skin stretched tight over his neck. He said nothing. He locked eyes with my boss, Lenny. He pointed at him. Then he rubbed his hands against his eyes as if he were crying. Then he mimed digging. Then he pretended he was rocking a baby. Then rage contorted his face and he slowly raised his finger to Lenny again. Then his face dropped back to neutral as he shambled away into the wavering heat. Lenny just laughed it off.

The next day we found poop in the staircase of the parking deck.

A few days later during lunch the office phone rang. It said TICKET OFFICE. It was one of the girls who worked there. She had just called UAPD because a homeless man was in the staircase yelling when she tried to go to her car. I already knew who it was, and I went out to see if the officers needed anything from me. When I went out, one of them was holding the Door Shitter by the arms trying to get the handcuffs on him. He was writhing and screaming gibberish. The other officer came to me and asked to be let in to use the phone. He was holding a pair of dirty blue jeans. They took the Door Shitter away.

For a week, anyway. On my drive to work I saw him by the off ramp. He didn't have a sign, like most people who stand there. He was just sitting on the guardrail. We made eye contact. The other doormen on the summer crew saw him, too. We knew it was somewhere, and it didn't take us long to find it. There are two cigarette trays outside. They're the kind only businesses have, with the sand in them. He had filled two of them up. I admit I was impressed. That was a lot of poop, especially for someone with such a sparse diet, as the Door Shitter's gaunt appearance suggested.

The police knew our problem, but there was little they could do. Despite increased patrols, we still found poop every few weeks for the next two months. Then it just stopped. We didn't see him around anymore. We agreed he probably moved on to create greener pastures. He maybe found a group to help him, or a job, or reconnected with a family member. Maybe he even migrated with the birds to avoid the winter, which is my own personal plan should things go south. These were all distractions, though, from the grimmer probabilities.

AKRON'S AUDIO
ALCHEMIST

By Andrew Poulsen

On a balmy Friday afternoon, I'm nervously careening through downtown Akron without my GPS, trying to prove I haven't lost my touch since leaving the "330." While craning my neck left and right down Main Street, I take in the living slideshow of industrial decay that is the city's downtown outskirts. Buildings by the score flank each side of the drag, each somehow more hollow and indistinct than the last. The only businesses with any signage or vestiges of a customer base are the handful of seedy strip clubs where even the most dimly lit corners of your mind couldn't brace you for the sad shenanigans that go on between their walls. This is the Akron I inherited, and its shell is tougher and coarser than ever.

I'm fifteen minutes early when I pull into an industrial park at the corner of West Bowery Street and Wooster Avenue. From the exterior, the building is just as faceless as the rest of the old brick warehouses that encircle downtown Akron. Pulling into the parking lot, I see a man sitting alone on a single wood pallet taking a drag from a cigarette, swirling the icy remains of a cold brew and staring at his iPhone, clad in slim-fit Levi's and a red V-neck T-shirt.

Most people passing by would assume this man to be a slightly aging barista trying to wind down on his fifteen. But to the inner-circle of the Akron music scene and to an endless horde of guitar nerds everywhere, I'm crashing the smoke break of Jamie Stillman. A part of many musical ventures, Jamie is best known as the founder of EarthQuaker Devices, a company that manufactures guitar effects pedals by hand and is quickly becoming one of the most ubiquitous names in the industry. What started as Jamie's solo basement hobby has exponentially evolved into a full-scale enterprise with more than thirty workers who help sell upwards of one hundred pedals a day all around the world.

For non-guitar-nerds, an effect pedal, or "stomp box," is a little device that alters the signal of an instrument to produce a particular sound effect. Pedals can work in a variety of ways—manipulating the sound wave of the instrument's signal, compressing it, or adding delays or speech variations. The use of stomp boxes first became popular in the mid-1960s, in the distorted, fuzzy guitar tones of the Who's "My Generation," and Rolling Stones hits like "(I Can't Get No) Satisfaction." While there's a sizable number of guitar purists who rely solely on their amplifiers to shape their tone, thousands of guitar players utilize effect pedals to create nearly every sound imaginable. And while a hundred pedals a day sounds minuscule when you consider the number of guitarists and pedal builders out in the world, Stillman is easily considered one of the leaders of the handmade, or "boutique," pedal movement of the past decade.

"I don't know QuickBooks, and I'm terrible at keeping receipts," Jamie says. "I don't really like talking on the phone. There was a time where I did everything, and I did it very DIY. I was always really good about emails. I got a reputation for answering emails at 3 a.m., because I would barely sleep. I just got so overwhelmed. It has totally outgrown me."

Hardly your everyday tycoon, Jamie puts out what's left of his American Spirit, greets me warmly and makes small talk as he prepares to show me the company's brand new, 15,000-square-foot facility. While he seems ecstatic with what he and his team have created over the past decade, he often carries an air that might best be described as an emotional cocktail of bewilderment, nervousness, and teetering optimism, like a recent lottery winner holding a huge cardboard check on the evening news.

"I've just always had low expectations," Jamie says. "By that, I mean that nothing I've ever done was meant to be something that would make me rich. I've always just pursued things I like doing and figured I would learn how to live off that."

Inside the warehouse at EarthQuaker's headquarters, stacks of boxes, unfamiliar equipment, and a small library's worth of files give away nothing about the sonically groundbreaking products made just one wall away. Jamie proudly pats the top of a CNC machine in excitement. While it might seem bizarre to see an Akron punk veteran so hyped up showing off a manufacturing tool, the computerized numerical control machine allows EarthQuaker to produce the pedals' enclosures, or housing, in-factory for the first time in its history, making the blank circuit boards the only pieces outsourced by the company.

As an almost lifelong guitarist, I had always imagined the production floor of a pedal company to be a messy and overwhelming cavalcade of noise, similar to a Sonic Youth record, or much worse, the Times Square Guitar Center, a dissonant audio orgy of teenagers and wannabes trading sloppy classic riffs on guitars and amps well out of their price range. But EarthQuaker's workshop is no different than any other in Akron's manufacturing district—it's polite and tidy, part code-abiding shop floor and part marketing agency.

About a dozen employees stand quietly at their stations, zapping and soldering complex arrangements of transistors and switches— or "lady bits" as they're known around the factory. The electronics are then enclosed in aluminum casing. After a pedal is built, each device is brought over to a long table and tested, as an employee plucks notes on a Gibson Les Paul running through a Fender Twin Reverb tube amplifier, to make sure each setting and modulation is up to Jamie's standards. From there, each pedal is boxed by hand and sent off to one of the countless distributors and dealers across the globe.

On the second floor of the building are a small number of pristine, freshly painted offices, most of which are still unfurnished from their move only a few weeks prior to my visit, in August of 2015. As Jamie leads me through each room, that air of the nervous lottery winner returns; we both seem to be pondering just how far this all seems from Jamie's days cutting his teeth in Kent's and Akron's DIY punk scenes.

Although the human element of EarthQuaker's building process is a source of pride for Jamie and others in the "boutique" (a term he uses begrudgingly) pedal market, it's the idea of putting friends to work and the unique sense of chemistry that comes from that camaraderie that Jamie believes defines the ethos of the company.

"It doesn't matter that much to me if something I buy was made by a human," says Jamie. "I just want to own a business where I can be a good employer and provide things like health insurance to people who wouldn't have it otherwise. Everyone who works here treats the business like they own it. They have a respect for the vision and the freedom to take it somewhere. Every one of us could be a representative of this company."

Born and raised in Kent, Jamie has always been a tinkerer. As we shared a seat on the wood pallet outside, he recalled memories of being five years old in his grandparents' backyard, dismantling an old jalopy or taking apart worn-out dining room furniture. It was around the same time that Jamie first discovered his love for music. He began as a drummer and eventually learned how to play guitar, which ultimately became his passion. Despite his lifelong obsession with music and understanding how things work, Jamie's modest nature allows him to dismiss himself as an armchair enthusiast of these crafts.

"I had this thing where I refused to really learn about the shit I was into," Jamie jokes. "I can pick up things quick, but as soon as I have to start reading about something, I'm bored to death. I can play guitar well and build a pedal, but I could never teach anyone those things or tell them exactly what I'm doing."

In his early teens, Jamie discovered punk rock, and he quickly became entrenched in the Kent and Akron DIY scenes, sneaking into shows and bars often with the likes of another notable Akron boy, Pat Carney, drummer for the Black Keys. Jamie laughs, thinking about how strange it is seeing his friend clad in a leather jacket on the cover of *Rolling Stone* when, in his memories, Jamie still sees the drummer as a 17 year old, whose lanky frame and thick glasses reflected less a rock-and-roll sex symbol and more Martin Starr's character, Bill Haverchuck, on *Freaks and Geeks*.

Throughout high school and into his 20s, Jamie played in a number of different punk bands and ran his own record label, Donut Friends. In the early 2000s, *Rolling Stone* gave the Black Keys a four-star review, which sparked a short-lived movement in the music industry where Akron had the major labels' attention in a way comparable to Nirvana-era Seattle. Jamie's own band, the Party of Helicopters, got a record deal that included an 18-month tour. But by his return, Jamie felt burned out on the band, which had already released six albums. In 2004, he took a job as a guitar technician for the Black Keys. It was around this time that he began tinkering with his own pedals and mastering the prototype that would become EarthQuaker's flagship product, the Hoof, a fuzz pedal derivative of the Sovtek Russian Green Big Muff which had become a key element in Black Keys guitarist Dan Auerbach's highly sought-after tone. The Sovtek was known for its massive, roaring capabilities, but also for its smoothness and clarity. A prime example is the sludgy opening riff off the band's 2003 single, "Thickfreakness."

Jamie watched his friends go from playing small clubs to basketball stadiums, but quit in 2011. The job had afforded him the time to develop his craft, letting him lay the foundation for what became EarthQuaker Devices. After photos appeared of Auerbach using Jamie's Hoof Fuzz on his pedal board on the guitar message boards online, Jamie's hobby began to turn into a business. Although Jamie was only known to the most esoteric of gear heads, Auerbach's subtle endorsement was hugely responsible for EarthQuaker's early sales.

"Pat and Dan have for sure had a hand in making this possible and giving me the time," Jamie says. He almost winces before he clarifies, "They're more important for the back end than being just a band that used our pedals. I didn't tell people for years that I was working for the Black Keys, because it's more validating that not everyone bought something just because I worked for them."

In 2008, Jamie quit his "real" job as a graphic designer to pursue EarthQuaker as a full-time endeavor. Jamie's wife Julie, a financial planner, gradually stepped in as the company's Vice President and took over running the business side of things, as it became apparent that Jamie's DIY accounting methods were less and less reasonable as the company boomed. EarthQuaker's product line continued to expand with another major staple in its fleet, the Disaster Transport, a delay pedal that emulates the vintage tape echo sounds of '60s and '70s psychedelic records, such as Pink Floyd's *Echoes*. The pedal sold so well that Jamie briefly discontinued it because he couldn't build them fast enough.

In 2010, Jamie finally hired his first employee, Jeff France, who is still the company's production manager. After France, the company began to add more builders—still working out of Jamie's basement. In 2012, EarthQuaker moved into its first production facility in an old glass factory in downtown Akron. But Jamie and company quickly outgrew that space, too. They now manufacture almost forty different pedals—from obnoxious, blown-out speaker fuzz boxes, to unholy church-organ simulators, to straight-up dad-rock overdrive, and hundreds of sonic possibilities in between. The company began hiring builders, designers, and operations team members nearly every six weeks. In the summer of 2015, Jamie and his staff of more than thirty workers moved into their current space not far from EarthQuaker's previous location, facing the University of Akron's campus.

"It's fun for me to experiment," Jamie says. "I'm fucking around until I find the thing that works. I was doing things with no real formal training, so it all sounded different and looked cooler than most things out there."

Today, Jamie is no longer fielding every email, call, and order like he did only a few years ago. When we sit to chat, he's visibly exhausted, having just returned from nearly a month on the road, visiting shops, making appearances at trade shows, and toting the brand to music gear elite. His role today resembles that of a visionary, or a disruptive business "wildcard," as Jamie would rather put it. I'd say he's like Steve Jobs on Xanax. While he is still always making his rounds across the shop floor, Jamie's staff covers many of the day-to-day operations, which affords him time to design pedals. Even with a fleet of stomp boxes that can emulate nearly any guitar tone imaginable, Jamie has a mental backlog of seven or eight models ready to be unleashed as soon as he can find the time. To Jamie, the success of it all harkens back to the golden years of industry in the early twentieth century, when prosperity could happen almost overnight with the right amount of luck.

"Sometimes this all gets lost on me," Jamie says. "This kind of thing just doesn't happen anymore. It feels like the '40s or '50s or something. With the record label and the band, I always operated on the idea that people would find me. But it never panned out until now."

Despite its ubiquity in the music community, EarthQuaker still hews to the DIY punk aesthetic on which Jamie was raised. Until 2012, Jamie was responsible for all the artwork on EarthQuaker pedals—nearly as famous as the sounds they produce. Much of that early artwork was inspired by the clip art found on punk zines, album artwork and show posters with its juxtaposed and often vulgar images and offset type.

"This all comes from being the graphic designer that I was," Jamie says. "I wasn't an illustrator, but I knew how to lay things out. Naming and designing the artwork used to be my favorite part about the process."

Each pedal's design aesthetic is very much the product of Jamie's racing mind. Some designs are geometric, like the Arpanoid, which transforms whatever you play into an arpeggiated scale like a synthesizer. Some are named after animals, such as the Hummingbird, a device which replicates the fluttery, stuttering tremolo effect heard on songs like "Crimson and Clover" by Tommy James and the Shondells, and represents the frenetic and manic nature of the eponymous bird.

"I like limitation," Jamie says. "I like to know the parameters. Almost to a fault, I like pedals to be tamed, but with the ability to be opened up. I like things to be taken far, but they always remain musical."

But it was the pedals that show Jamie's Ohio roots that resonated with me when I first discovered the company. Several EarthQuaker names derive from various Ohio landmarks. The Terminal Fuzz bears an outline of Cleveland's Terminal Tower and delivers a gritty, blown-speaker tone that most would believe captures the city's coarse and industrial aesthetic. The aforementioned Disaster Transport is named after the classic Cedar Point indoor roller coaster my brother and I flocked to because it never had a line and they always pumped the air conditioning. Some references are more personal. The Palisades is named after a street on Akron's west side, near Highland Square, where Jamie and his wife used to live.

As far as advertising and self-promotion, Jamie tore a page from the book of his idols Led Zeppelin, whom many forget built their commercial success without the support of radio play. "I like the idea of building a mystique," Jamie says, half-jokingly. Most of Earth-Quaker's early success relied on word-of-mouth and online forums. The company didn't pay for its first magazine ad until 2012, after the company had already entered the conversation among top boutique pedal builders. Even so, its advertisements are very minimal, revealing only the name of the pedal and the city in which it is built. Whereas most music equipment companies heavily rely on pimping out the big name artists who use their gear, plastering them on every ad and landing page, Jamie has always felt uneasy about trumpeting the artists who use his pedals. Besides the Black Keys, EarthQuaker Devices have been used by musical heavyweights from Modest Mouse to Coldplay to Brad Paisley to the Mars Volta—Jamie stopped keeping track long ago. Taking another long drag of a cigarette, he mentions a time he built a custom fuzz pedal for Bruno Mars, an artist about whom he knew nothing until seeing his face on a magazine while on a flight.

"I just always thought it was kind of gross to see a guy in an ad that's like, 'So and so uses this product to get the best tone,'" Jamie says, in an affected ad-man voice. "I would never do something like that."

Jamie's resistance to aggressive, superfluous ads and endorsements isn't just about adhering to his punk rock convictions. Companies like EarthQuaker work in a very saturated market, where they can easily get pigeonholed by customers who believe their products only serve a certain genre or sound. A major part of EarthQuaker's success has come from its broad appeal and tonal accessibility. Artists like Bruno Mars can use a Hoof Fuzz to replicate the crunch of '70s rock and roll, while the Mars Volta might use a more extreme effect to evoke space ships or an industrial breakdown. There are plenty of innovative and experimental companies that make pedals more raucous and dissonant than anything EarthQuaker would ever put to market, but they often only find success among the most esoteric noisemakers. Trying to define what EarthQuaker is about from a tonal standpoint is almost like trying to define what music itself is about. From these little metal boxes come sounds for practically every player.

"I don't want anyone coming with any preconceived notions about us," Jamie says. "It's an insult to those who make more experimental noise pedals and take it seriously. We would never put out something that you couldn't tame."

The success of EarthQuaker Devices is both symbolic and paradoxical. Aside from a certain St. Vincent-St. Mary High School small forward, what have been the two most significant exports the city has produced? The first is undoubtedly industry. Rubber put food on the table for many of my ancestors, and thousands upon thousands of other Akronites can say the same. Schools and streets bear the names of the men who gave the city its power, leaving their exhausted scraps collapsed and broken all around the city.

The second most important export is a little more up for debate, but most would agree that Akron has pumped out an exceptional number of talented musicians for its relatively small size. Along with Akron's current favorite sons, the Black Keys, art rock heroes Devo, groundbreaking front woman Chrissie Hynde, and even the late Jani Lane who penned the 1990 hair metal smash, "Cherry Pie," all entered superstardom by way of the Rubber City.

So, what happened?

Well, let's put it this way: I'm 23 years old and the very thing that gave this city an identity has turned its nickname into a two-decade-old misnomer. As far as the rock stars it's delivered, all packed up for bigger markets. Chrissie Hynde dropped out of Kent State's art school and found fame overseas when she formed the Pretenders in London. The Black Keys famously moved to Nashville in 2011 as they made their push towards becoming the stadium-filling, cover-modeling, blues-rock outfit we know them as now.

So, what's left when the lapdogs of industry fetch another bone and another rising slugger in the minors gets called up to The Show? On the surface, it's a lot of empty, depressing buildings and even more depressing stories of "I saw them when..." But such is the circle of life. And death and decay can often make ground more fertile for rebirth.

"People always ask me to describe Akron," Jamie says. "I think it's a dead city trying to come back, and it's getting to a point where it's getting a focus."

Jamie's vision has glued together the broken bones of these two factors that once made Akron great. Without getting too hyperbolic, EarthQuaker is a proverbial phoenix, operating literally in the decay of a dead factory. And Jamie's pedals have made him an unintentional ambassador and evangelist amongst musicians the world over for a city he never thought would've been so critical in his success.

"Bands come here now because they know that EarthQuaker is here," Jamie says. "They end up really liking it here, which surprises me, because I've been here my whole life, so my mind isn't blown driving to a national park in ten minutes."

But the Akron hype and curiosity isn't a total accident. Whereas many pedal companies downplay where they're headquartered, each EarthQuaker box, advertisement and instruction manual bears the city's name, often in the form of a cheeky phrase like "Made in the gilded cloud of Akron, Ohio." For Jamie, the Akron appreciation has grown over time. Looking back on the success he's achieving, he and his team know they're in a pretty lonely winner's circle for producers in any industry, let alone among companies making handmade goods.

"There's hardly anything in our industry that has been as successful as we have that still does stuff here," Jamie says. "I don't think the city recognizes just how widespread our stuff is or how successful we are."

Jamie doesn't blame artists or businesspeople for skipping town to pursue bigger dreams in bigger cities, and he admits that EarthQuaker on paper is probably better suited for New York, Los Angeles, or Nashville. But despite the number of signs indicating that EarthQuaker could one day outgrow Akron as it has outgrown Jamie's basement, he assures me that that he doesn't see the company ever leaving the city.

"Akron makes this possible," Jamie says. "We could never afford to do this in those larger cities. Julie and I really like living here and the community we have here. Plus, all the people who work here live here—and we couldn't survive without them."

Even with all the talk of enterprise, expansion, distribution, and recognition, Jamie still has a Midwestern earnestness and sincerity that harken back to a guy soldering circuit boards in his boxers a decade ago.

EarthQuaker needs Akron, but Akron also needs EarthQuaker. In a city that's always been the launch pad and never the stratosphere, it's rare to find a company painstakingly pushing itself to its creative and production limits without leaving home.

It's almost five o'clock, and nearly the entire company has gone home. Wrapping up our interview, Jamie leans forward, grinding the ash of his last cigarette into the asphalt. His workday isn't over, and despite no longer carrying the entire load, I see the "answers emails at 3 a.m." Jamie – he seems anxious to get back to work. We shake hands, name drop a few fellow Akronites, and Jamie sends me off with one final laugh that solidifies how seriously he takes himself as a musical magnate.

"I'm almost forty, and I've been living off the assumption that I'm still fifteen years old. I don't think much has changed. I just did something that finally worked...and I got fatter."

Driving home, I keep thinking about Jamie's comment. What did I expect? Did I think that instead of sharing Akron tales on a wood pallet I'd be across some reclaimed oak desk, while some megalomaniac visionary strokes his ego while simultaneously browbeating a cowardly assistant into fetching us two iced mochas? Of course not. After all, Jamie arranged this interview personally, no assistant necessary.

But it seems uncommon to meet someone so popular in his business with so much humility. So much caution. Sure, EarthQuaker Devices makes boutique effect pedals. To the world at large that doesn't mean much. Jamie's not putting planes in the sky or helping lonely singles find "love" by swiping their thumbs across their phone. But whether the world knows it, it has heard the fruits of Jamie's labor. On recordings heard by millions and at live shows witnessed by thousands, the sonic alchemy of EarthQuaker Devices has rung in the ears of so many, at the hands of some of music's biggest stars. That kind of impact might actually warrant a little ego-stroking and assistant-browbeating.

However, as I take in a last eyeful of Akron's beige and gray downtown, a question dawns on me: is there a place more fertile for traits of humility and caution than this city? If history has taught Akron anything, it's that success guarantees nothing and the well of good fortune can run dry at any moment. Growing up surrounded by so many boarded-up factories and storefronts gives Akronites an inherent humility. A whiff of mortality.

Jamie isn't naive about his commercial success or the résumés of his customers. His punk rock roots and Midwest upbringing just allow him to see it differently. Success isn't a goal, but a means. A means to still get to rock out in dirty bars with your buddies on the weekends while comfortably providing for a family. A means to explore your creative vision and take it as far as you can, while being able to share it with those who cared long before you had them on your payroll.

Maybe going corporate wasn't the worst thing to happen to this Akron punk.

CONFESSIONS OF A RUST BELT ORPHAN
(OR HOW I LEARNED TO STOP WORRYING AND LOVE AKRON)

By Jason Segedy

Go to sleep, Captain Future, in your lair of art deco
You were our pioneer of progress, but tomorrow's been postponed
Go to sleep, Captain Future, let corrosion close your eyes
If the board should vote to restore hope, we'll pass along the lie
– The Secret Sound of the NSA, "Captain Future"

In the Beginning...

As near as I can tell, the term "Rust Belt" originated sometime in the mid-1980s. That sounds about right.

I originated slightly earlier, in 1972, at St. Thomas Hospital in Akron, Ohio, Rubber Capital of the World. My very earliest memory is of a day, sometime in the summer of 1975, that my parents, my baby brother, and I went on a camping trip to Lake Milton, just west of Youngstown. I was three years old. To this day, I have no idea why, of all of the things that I could remember, but don't, I happen to remember this one. But it is a good place to start.

The memory is so vivid that I can still remember looking at the green overhead freeway signs along the West Expressway in Akron. Some of the signs were in kilometers as well as in miles back then, due to an ill-fated attempt to convert Americans to the metric system in the 1970s. I remember the overpoweringly pungent smell of rubber wafting from the smokestacks of B.F. Goodrich and Firestone. I recall asking my mother about it, and her explaining that those were the factories where the tires, and the rubber, and the chemicals were made. They were made by hard-working, good people—people like my Uncle Jim. But more on that later.

When I was a little bit older, I would learn that this was the smell of good jobs; of hard, dangerous work; and of the way of life that built the modern version of this quirky and gritty town. It was the smell that tripled Akron's population between 1910 and 1920, transforming it from a sleepy former canal town to the thirty-second largest city in America. It is a smell laced with melancholy, ambivalence, and nostalgia—for it was the smell of an era that was quickly coming to an end (although I was far too young to be aware of this fact at the time). It was sometimes the smell of tragedy.

We stopped by my grandparents' house, in Firestone Park, on the way to the campground. I can still remember my grandmother giving me a box of Barnum's Animals crackers for the road. She was always kind and generous like that.

Who were my grandparents? My grandparents were Akron. It's as simple as that. Their story was Akron's story. My grandfather, George Segedy, was born in 1916, in Barnesboro, a small coal-mining town in Western Pennsylvania, somewhere between Johnstown, DuBois, and nowhere. His father, a coal miner, had emigrated there from Hungary nine years earlier. My grandmother, Helen Szabo, was born in Barberton, in 1920. Barberton was reportedly the most-industrialized city in the United States, per capita, at some point around that time.

They were both factory workers for their entire working lives (I don't think they called jobs like that "careers" back then). My grandfather worked at the Firestone Tire & Rubber Company. My grandmother worked at Saalfield Publishing, a factory that was one of the largest producers of children's books, games, and puzzles in the world. Today, both of the plants where they worked form part of a gutted, derelict, post-apocalyptic moonscape in South Akron, located between that same West Expressway and perdition. The City of Akron has plans for revitalizing this former industrial area. It needs to happen, but there are ghosts there.

My name is Ozymandias, King of Kings,
Look on my works, ye Mighty, and despair!
Nothing beside remains. Round the decay
Of that colossal wreck, boundless and bare
The lone and level sands stretch far away.
– Percy Bysshe Shelley, "Ozymandias"

My grandparents' house exemplified what it was to live in working-class Akron in the late 1970s and early 1980s. My stream-of-consciousness memories of that house include: lots of cigarettes and ashtrays; *Hee-Haw; The Joker's Wild*; fresh tomatoes and peppers; Fred & Lamont Sanford; Archie & Edith Bunker; Herb Score and Indians baseball on the radio on the front porch; hand-knitted afghans; cold cans of Coca-Cola and Pabst Blue Ribbon; the Ohio Lottery; chicken and *galuskas* (dumplings); a garage floor that you could eat off of; a meticulously maintained fourteen-year-old Chrysler with 29,000 miles on it; a refrigerator in the dining room because the kitchen was too small; catching fireflies in jars; and all being right with the world.

I always associate the familiar comfort of that tiny two-bedroom bungalow with the omnipresence of cigarette smoke and television. I remember sitting there on May 18, 1980. It was my eighth birthday. We were sitting in front of the TV, watching coverage of the Mount St. Helens eruption in Washington State. I remember talking about the fact that it was going to be the year 2000 (The Future!) in just twenty years. I remember thinking about the fact that I would be twenty-eight years old then, and how inconceivably distant it all seemed. Things seem so permanent when you're eight, and time moves ever-so-slowly.

More often than not, when we visited my grandparents, my Uncle Jim and Aunt Helen would be there. Uncle Jim was born in 1936, in West Virginia. His family, too, had come to Akron to find work that was better-paying, steadier, and less dangerous than the work in the coal mines. Uncle Jim was a rubber worker, first at Mohawk Rubber and then later at B.F. Goodrich. Uncle Jim also cut hair over at the most-appropriately named West Virginia Barbershop, on South Arlington Street in East Akron. He was one of the best, most decent, kindest people that I have ever known.

I remember asking my mother once why Uncle Jim never washed his hands. She scolded me, explaining that he did wash his hands, but that because he built tires, his hands were stained with carbon black, which wouldn't come out no matter how hard you scrubbed. I learned later that it would take about six months for that stuff to leach out of your pores once you quit working.

Uncle Jim died in 1983, killed in an industrial accident on the job at B.F. Goodrich. He was only forty-seven. The plant would close for good about a year later.

It was an unthinkably tragic event, at a singularly traumatic time for Akron. It was the end of an era.

Times Change

My friend Della Rucker wrote a great post entitled, "The Elder Children of the Rust Belt," over at her blog, *Wise Economy*. It dredged up all of these old memories, and it got me thinking about childhood, about this place that I love, and about the experience of growing up just as an economic era (perhaps the most prosperous and anomalous one in modern history) was coming to an end.

That is what the late 1970s and early 1980s was: the end of one thing, and the beginning of (a still yet-to-be-determined) something else. I didn't know it at the time, but that's because I was just a kid.

In retrospect it was obvious: the decay; the deterioration, the decomposition, the slow-at-first, and then faster-than-you-can-see-it unwinding of an industrial machine that had been wound up far, far, too tight. The machine runs until it breaks down; then it is replaced with a new and more efficient one—a perfectly ironic metaphor for an industrial society that killed the goose that laid the golden egg. It was a machine made up of unions, and management, and capitalized sunk costs, and supply chains, and commodity prices, and globalization.

Except it wasn't really a machine at all. It was really just people. And people aren't machines. When they are treated as such, and then discarded as obsolete, there are consequences. You could hear it in the music: from the decadent, desperately-seeking-something (escape) pulse of disco, to the (first) nihilistic and (then) fatalistic sound of punk and post-punk. It's not an accident that a band called Devo came from Akron, Ohio. De-evolution: the idea that instead of evolving, mankind has actually regressed, as evidenced by the dysfunction and herd mentality of American society. It sounded a lot like Akron in the late 1970s. It still sounds a little bit like the Rust Belt today.

As an adult, looking back at the experience of growing up at that time, you realize how much it colors your thinking and outlook on life. It's all the more poignant when you realize that the "end-of-an-era" is never really an "end" as such, but is really a transition to something else. But to what exactly?

The end of that era, which was marked by strikes, layoffs, and unemployment, was followed by its echoes and repercussions—economic dislocation, outmigration, poverty, and abandonment—as well as the more intangible psychological detritus: the pains from the phantom limb long after the amputation, the vertiginous sensation of watching someone (or something) die.

And it came to me then
That every plan
Is a tiny prayer to Father Time
As I stared at my shoes
In the ICU
That reeked of piss and 409
It sung like a violent wind
That our memories depend
On a faulty camera in our minds
'Cause there's no comfort in the waiting room
Just nervous paces bracing for bad news
Love is watching someone die...
– Death Cab For Cutie, "What Sarah Said"

But it is both our tragedy and our glory that life goes on.

Della raised a lot of these issues in her post: our generation's ambivalent relationship with the American Dream (like Della, I feel the same unpleasant taste of rust in my mouth whenever I write or utter that phrase); our distrust of organizations and institutions; and our realization that you have to keep going, fight, and survive, in spite of it all. She talked about how we came of age at a time of loss: "not loss like a massive destruction, but a loss like something insidious, deep, pervasive."

It is so true, and it is so misunderstood. One of the people commenting on her blog post said, essentially, that it is dangerous to romanticize about a "golden age," that all generations struggle, and that life is hard.

Yes, those things are all true. But they are largely irrelevant to the topic at hand.

There is a very large middle ground between a "golden age" and an "existential struggle." The time and place about which we are both writing (the late 1970s through the present, in the Rust Belt) is neither. But it is undoubtedly a time of extreme transition. It is a great economic unraveling, and we are collectively and individually still trying to figure out how to navigate through it, survive it, and ultimately build something better out of it.

History is cyclical. Regardless of how enamored Americans, in general, may be with the idea, it is not linear. It is neither a long, slow march toward utopia, nor toward oblivion. When I look at history, I see times of relative (and it's all relative, this side of paradise) peace, prosperity, and stability; and other times of relative strife, economic upheaval, uncertainty, and instability. We really did move from one of those times to the other, beginning in the 1970s, and continuing through the present.

The point that is easy to miss when uttering phrases like "life is hard for every generation" is that none of this discussion about the Rust Belt—where it's been, where it is going—has anything to do with a "golden age." But it has everything to do with the fact that this time of transition was an era (like all eras) that meant a lot (good and bad) to the people that lived through it. It helped make them who they are today, and it helped make where they live what it is today.

For those who were kids at the time the great unraveling began (people like me, and people like Della), it is partially about the narrative that we were socialized to believe in at a very young age, and how that narrative went up in a puff of smoke. In 1977, I could smell rubber in the air, and many of my family members and friends' parents worked in rubber factories. In 1982, the last passenger tire was built in Akron. By 1984, 90% of those jobs were gone, many of those people had moved out of town, and the whole thing was already a fading memory.

Just as when a person dies, many people reacted with a mixture of silence, embarrassment, and denial. As a kid, especially, you construct your identity based upon the place in which you live. The whole identity that I had built, even as a small child, was of a proud Akronite: *This is the* **RUBBER CAPITAL OF THE WORLD***; this is where we make lots and lots of* **Useful Things** *for people all over the* *world; this is where **Real Americans Do Real Work**; this is where people from Europe, the South, and Appalachia come to make a **Better Life** for themselves...*

Well, that all got yanked away. I couldn't believe any of those things anymore, because they were no longer true, and I knew it. I could see it with my own two eyes. Maybe some of them were never true to begin with, but kids can't live a lie the way that adults can. When the mythology of your hometown no longer stands up to scrutiny, it can be jarring and disorienting. It can even be heartbreaking.

We're the middle children of history, man. No purpose or place. We have no Great War. No Great Depression. Our great war is a spiritual war. Our great depression is our lives.
– Tyler Durden, "Fight Club"

I'm fond of the above quote. I was even fonder of it when I was 28 years old. Time, and the realization that life is short, and that you ultimately have to participate and do something with it besides analyze it as an outside observer, has lessened its power considerably. It remains the quintessential Generation X quote, from the quintessential Generation X movie. It certainly fits in quite well with all of this. But, then again, maybe it shouldn't.

I use the phrase "Rust Belt Orphan" in the title of this piece, because that is what the experience of coming of age at the time of the great economic unraveling feels like at the gut level. But it's a dangerous and unproductive combination, when coupled with the whole Gen-X thing.

In many ways, the Rust Belt is the "Generation X" of regions— the place that just doesn't seem to fit in; the place that most people would just as soon forget about; the place that would, in fact, just as soon forget about itself; the place that, if it does dare to acknowledge its own existence or needs, barely notices the surprised frowns of displeasure and disdain from those on the outside, because they have already been subsumed by the place's own self-doubt and self-loathing.

A fake chinese rubber plant
In the fake plastic earth
That she bought from a rubber man
In a town full of rubber plans
To get rid of itself
– Radiohead, "Fake Plastic Trees"

The whole Gen-X misfit wandering-in-the-Rust Belt-wilderness meme is a palpably prevalent, but seldom-acknowledged part of our regional culture. It is probably just as well. It's so easy for the whole smoldering heap of negativity to degenerate into a viscous morass of alienation and anomie. Little good can come from going any further down that dead-end road.

Whither the Future?

The Greek word for "return" is nostos. Algos means "suffering." So nostalgia is the suffering caused by an unappeased yearning to return.
– Milan Kundera, "Ignorance"

So where does this all leave us?

First, as a region, I think we have to get serious about making our peace with the past and moving on. We have begun to do this in Akron, and, if the stories and anecdotal evidence are to be believed, we are probably ahead of the region as a whole.

But what does "making our peace" and "moving on" really mean? In many ways, I think our region has been going through a collective period of mourning for the better part of four decades. Nostalgia and angst over what has been lost (some of our identity, prosperity, and national prominence) is all part of the grieving process. The best way out is always through.

But we should grieve—not so we can wallow in the experience and refuse to move on, but so we can gain a better understanding of who we are and where we come from. Coming to grips with and acknowledging those things ultimately enables us to help make these places that we love better.

We Americans are generally not all that good at, or comfortable with, mourning or grief. There's a very American idea that grieving is synonymous with "moving on" and (even worse) that "moving on" is synonymous with "getting over it."

We're very comfortable with that neat and tidy, straight, upwardly trending line toward the future (and a more prosperous, progressive, and enlightened future it will always be, world without end, Amen).

We're not so comfortable with that messy and confusing historical cycle of boom-and-bust, of evolution and de-evolution, of creation and destruction and reinvention. But that's the world as we actually experience it, and it's the one that we must live in. It is far from perfect. But for all of its trials and tribulations, the world that we inhabit has one big advantage: it is real.

"Moving on" means refusing to become paralyzed by the past, living up to our present responsibilities, and striving every day to become the type of people who are better able to help others. But "moving on" doesn't mean that we forget about the past, that we pretend that we didn't experience what we did, or that we create an alternate reality to avoid playing the hand that we've actually been dealt.

Second, I don't think we can, or should, "get over" the Rust Belt. The very phrase "get over it" traffics in denial, wishful thinking, and the estrangement of one's self from one's roots. Countless attempts to "get over" the Rust Belt have resulted in the innumerable short-sighted, "get rich quick" economic development projects, and public-private pyramid schemes that many of us have come to find so distasteful, ineffective, and expensive.

We don't have to be (and can't be, even if we want to) something that we are not. But we do have to be the best place that we can be. This might mean that we are a smaller, relatively less-prominent place. But it also means that we can be a much better connected, more cohesive, coherent, and equitable place. The only people who can stop us from becoming that place are ourselves.

For a place that has been burned so badly by the vicissitudes of the global economy, big business, and big industry, we always seem to be so quick to put our faith in the Next Big Project, the Next Big

Organization, and the Next Big Thing. I'm not sure whether this is the cause of our current economic malaise, or the effect, or both. Whatever it is, we need to stop doing it.

Does this mean that we should never do or dream anything big? No. Absolutely not. But it does mean that we should be prudent and wise, and that we should prefer our economic development and public investment to be hyper-nimble, hyper-scalable, hyper-neighborhood-focused, and ultra-diverse. Fetishizing urban designer Daniel Burnham's famous quote—"Make no little plans, for they have no magic to stir men's blood"—has done us much harm. Sometimes "little plans" are exactly what we need, because they often involve fundamentals, are easier to pull off, and more readily establish trust, inspire hope, and build relationships.

Those of us who came of age during the great economic unraveling and (still painful) transition from the Great American Manufacturing Belt to the Rust Belt might just be in a better position to understand our challenges, and to find the creative solutions required to meet them head-on. Those of us who stuck it out and still live here, know where we came from. We're under no illusions about who we are or where we live. I think Della Rucker was on to something when she listed what we can bring to the table:

- Determination
- Long-game focus
- Understanding the depth of the pit and the long way left to climb out of it
- Resourcefulness
- Ability to salvage
- Expectation that there are no easy answers
- Disinclination to believe that everything will be all right if only we do this One Big Thing

When I look at this list, I see pragmatism, resilience, self-knowledge, survival skills, and leadership. It all rings true.

He wanted to care, and he could not care. For he had gone away and he could never go back any more. The gates were closed, the sun was gone down, and there was no beauty but the gray beauty of steel that withstands all time. Even the grief he could have borne was left behind in the country of illusion, of youth, of the richness of life, where his winter dreams had flourished.

"Long ago," he said, "long ago, there was something in me, but now that thing is gone. Now that thing is gone, that thing is gone. I cannot cry. I cannot care. That thing will come back no more."
– F. Scott Fitzgerald, "Winter Dreams"

So, let's have our final elegy for the Rust Belt. Then, let's get to work.

RIP, UNKNOWN SKELETAL REMAINS

By Jennifer Conn

The dirt path to the Summit County potter's field in Tallmadge, Ohio, no longer winds through a stretch of emerald woods heavy in summer with blackberries and tangled with thistle, brambles and vines. It doesn't end at the back of the shimmering field that once masked the gated entrance to the cemetery. The path no longer feels like a portal to a secret. It's my secret—although, in truth, it's a secret shared with many long-dead souls.

For me, walking into that cool, green space always brought immediate comfort, like letting out breath held too long. Woods have always been home to me, but a woods concealing a forgotten cemetery was a gift to a teen who needed time and space to brood. I sometimes wrote while I was there, poetry, story ideas, characters' names. There were never voices on the wind or visions from beyond the veil. But I felt a complete sense of belonging at the potter's field; an understanding that I was always welcome there, perhaps by some energy pleased to be acknowledged. Leaving always saddened me. It made me feel strangely exposed.

That was during the decades the potter's field was tucked away off the sprawling grounds of the Summit County Home in Tallmadge. The home was a majestic, classic revival-style structure we locals just called the "old folks home."

Today, the graveyard has become a kind of accidental roadside attraction. In 2008, the path through the woods to the gates was closed. Stripped of its secrecy, the cemetery entrance is now next to a trail built by the Summit Metro Parks, which cuts through the sheared remnants of what was once the field.

The potter's field still stands open, silently inviting people to step in. But I've watched visitors pass by those gates without turning their heads, as the cemetery is unmarked. It makes me ashamed that we seem to be losing touch with yet another feature of our human connectedness—honoring our dead.

In fairness, if you aren't paying attention you likely don't notice the three lone headstones. Two, standing back-to-back, are identical, inscribed, "John Keck, 1847–1935," and "Constantina Plarinos, 1865–1935." I think of them as lovers who perished together, maybe of some old-time illness like scarlet fever or tuberculosis. The only other marker

in the cemetery is a flat, bronze plaque inscribed, "Rest in Peace Unknown Skeletal Remains, Summit County Ohio."

But even those who walk through the gates and realize they're standing in an old burial site would not understand that more than 900 people who once called this area home are buried there. Our great-great-grandmas and grandpas along with distant cousins and drifters rest in that potter's field.

And not that long ago, there was a way to know who was in each plot. Now the dead are nearly impossible to identify.

The Summit County Home

Growing up in Cuyahoga Falls, we told ghost stories about the old folks home. It was built nearly a century ago on Route 91, with the potter's field in the adjacent woods. Everyone knew a cemetery was somewhere on the grounds, but in all the visits I made to it, I never saw another living soul.

I remember a few neighborhood kids claiming they'd snuck inside the building after dark and watched the ghost of a woman in a long, white gown gliding down the master staircase. To us, it had always just been there, spreading out darkly on its hill; a beautiful Goliath, forbidding, silent and ripe for a haunting.

In truth, the home operated from 1919 until 1970, and only stood crumbling and empty until about 1980. It was then demolished and replaced with a modern nursing and rehabilitation facility that caused it to fade from local legend.

But it wasn't until 1988 that Summit County finally erected a tall marble monument at the site of the former old folks home, memorializing those buried in the potter's field. The inscription explains the site was used from 1916 to 1948 to bury the indigent elderly and people who ended up at the home "due to unfortunate reasons caused by the Depression and difficult times." The monument also tells of a millhouse on the grounds that burned down in 1981, destroying the records of everyone buried there, explaining why most the graves are unmarked.

But some locals suspect differently, as the list of those buried there surfaced more than once. And, other records show many of those buried in the potter's field never lived at the home—they were reinterred from two other area cemeteries.

The Summit County Infirmary

When the Summit County Home was built in 1916, it replaced the Summit County Infirmary, a poorhouse and working farm built in

1864 in West Akron. Not an actual hospital, the Summit County Infirmary, located at West Exchange Street and Rose Boulevard, housed poor families with children; people considered insane or very ill; and the indigent elderly. It too housed a cemetery, known simply as the pauper's cemetery.

When the infirmary closed in 1919, it ended decades of abuse and mistreatment of its residents, both living and dead. In *Wicked Akron: Tales of Rumrunners, Mobsters and Other Rubber City Rogues*, Kymberli Hagelberg wrote about the infirmary's physician, Alvin K. Fouser, who was accused in the late 1800s of robbing the paupers' graves and selling bodies for $5 to medical researchers. Fouser was never formally charged, but the accusation sparked further investigations. Other unsavory activities were uncovered, which led to the infirmary's closure.

But the property it occupied was valuable. *Past Pursuits*, a publication of the Akron-Summit County Public Library, recounts that in July 1912, a buyer proposed to purchase the infirmary property with a single stipulation—that the pauper's cemetery be removed.

The Beacon Journal reported the infirmary and grounds were sold in 1916, and in 1919, all living residents were moved to the new Summit County Home. No mention was made of the 209 bodies in the infirmary's pauper's cemetery. They were believed to have been moved to the Summit County Home, but many likely were not. In 2005, construction crews working near the West Akron Infirmary site were told to be on the lookout for human remains.

Cemetery records lost—and found

When I first became interested in writing about the potter's field, I met local historian Marilyn Kovatch, a charter member of the Summit County Genealogical Society who twice served as chapter president. She was passionate about genealogy and the area's history, and she clearly appreciated my interest, opening her archives and introducing me to locals with first-hand information. Mrs. Kovatch shared everything she knew about the home and the potter's field, including meticulously organized news clippings, records, and resident accounts.

One article from the *Beacon Journal* had been handled so often the date was illegible. It quoted a man working in Akron in 1982 under the federal Comprehensive Employment and Training Act program who said his crew had found a copy of the potter's field burial records downtown in the old Akron Armory when it was being torn down. He said his supervisors instructed the crew to not only throw away the records but to also remove and throw away the numbered porcelain markers from the graves that coincided with them.

In destroying the numbered markers, there would never again be a way to identify the bodies in any of the graves at the burial site.

I remember asking Mrs. Kovatch why workers would have been told to do such a thing. Grave robbery, she had answered. So someone could steal the few valuables—wedding rings and gold teeth—those poor people had left in the world. It was not uncommon, she said, with older, forgotten cemeteries.

I was astonished. I still cannot understand how anyone could perform such an act without fear of karma smiting their asses or, at the very least, of their own conscience eventually driving them mad.

Not long after that article was published, a former employee of the Summit County Welfare office, who wished to remain anonymous, contacted Mrs. Kovatch with a similar story. The woman said she had found a copy of the same burial records twenty-five years earlier in a wastebasket in a downtown Akron office, but she had kept them. Mrs. Kovatch knew as soon as she saw the documents they were the burial records from the potter's field. When Mrs. Kovatch handed the records to me to copy, it felt like I'd been given a treasure map.

Hand-written in ledger form, the records provide the deceased's name and age if known, as well as the grave and permit number—the numbers corresponding to the markers thrown away by the federal worker's crew. The records also list the undertaker's name and sometimes remarks, including any unusual information surrounding the person's death. I pored over the records for weeks, examining the neat script, imagining the subjects' faces and wishing them peace.

Some of the homeless or possibly drifters are listed this way: "unknown man, March 10, 1917, shot on the high level bridge;" "unknown man, March 10, 1917, shot on the high level bridge;" "unknown man, September 21, 1920, bullet hole in chest;" and "unknown man, July 27, 1917, found in river, Falls." Nicknames also were noted, including "Bumblebee" and "Dog Face." Sometimes the notations are curious, such as "Jim Douglas, November 3, 1925, buried, removed same day." One notable remark is found under the listing of John Kisey, buried October 31, 1919: "First body buried in the new cemetery, rained all day."

Over the years, Mrs. Kovatch's information has drawn me back, again and again, to the potter's field and to further research. I realize now how much the inscription on the monument must have troubled her. There might have been a fire, but the records were not destroyed in it. But without the porcelain grave markers, the records may be impossible to match with the gravesites.

I recently tried to contact Mrs. Kovatch to share new information I'd found, but was saddened to learn she died in 1999. An *Akron Beacon Journal* obituary praised her work and quoted genealogical society member Frances Musson saying, "She was a marvelous genealogist. She worked so hard on getting the cemeteries recorded and getting the deaths and all the different transactions recorded, from the courthouse to anyplace she could find them."

She was indeed a force for lost souls. It was her calling.

Four Pines Cemetery

Among the reasons genealogists like Mrs. Kovatch preserve historic records is because cemeteries too often feel like Brothers Grimm tales. They can take people seeking lost relatives on a difficult and distressing journey.

For those buried in the potter's field, the plot thickens. Prior to the opening of the Summit County site, and possibly after the Summit County Infirmary closed, there was once another cemetery in Tallmadge, not far, as the crow flies, from the existing potter's field. This older burial ground was marked by four pine trees standing near the Howe Road entrance to the Summit County Fairgrounds. One of the pines still stands.

Older Tallmadge residents believe this cemetery was used as an interim burial ground while the Summit County Home was under construction. Once the home was complete, the bodies from the "four pines" cemetery were moved to the potter's field.

But, according to an old-timer I spoke with in the '90s, the pine-marked cemetery might have been even older. He said that as a child in the early 1900s, he watched from his family's farmhouse window as morticians drove a horse and wagon up the narrow dirt cow path that is now Howe Road, in harsh weather, to dump the bodies, sans caskets, off the side of the wagon rather than make the laborious trip up the hill in the mud or snow to the cemetery. The morticians, paid $5 a body and $5 a casket to carry the deceased to the burial ground, were thought to have kept the $5.

The old man's tale bears truth. In 1981, a highway project to widen Howe Road from two lanes to four unearthed human bones near the fairgrounds. A *Tallmadge Express* story reported the bones were likely those of Summit County Home residents who had been buried in the obscure little cemetery near the fairgrounds. An Ohio Department of Transportation project map shows a cemetery in that vicinity.

Clearly, like those left behind at the Summit County Infirmary, not all the remains at the obscure pine-marked cemetery made it to the potter's field.

The bones released during the Howe Road project were later reinterred at the potter's field. Memorialized only as "Unknown Skeletal Remains," they joined the hundreds of other area residents who became anonymous in death through no fault of their own.

Potter's Field Records Preserved

The last time I visited the potter's field, limp, sun-bleached flags honoring the cemetery's veterans hung at the entrance. The grounds seemed more uneven, patterned with a rugged grid of roots from the old trees that keep the place in perpetual shade. Poison ivy climbed everywhere.

The cemetery remains obscure because the huge marble monument at the site of the Summit County Home was never moved to the new entrance in the Tallmadge Metro Park. The monument stands,

fully concealed by the woods, next to a parking lot for the new facility that's at the site of the old home.

The monument is as untethered to its purpose as, in the end, the potter's field residents are to their identities, and their loved ones.

But even though time and human failings have done much to diminish the old cemetery, there is some satisfaction in knowing that even a few of the 900 people buried in obscurity in the Summit County potter's field might yet be found by their loved ones. Mrs. Kovatch saw to it that those lost-and-then-found handwritten burial records, titled "Summit County Ohio Infirmary & Miscellaneous Records 1916 to 1952," were given to the Special Collections Division of the Akron-Summit County Public Library for safekeeping, along with the book *Lest We Forget*, which provides Summit County burial records and other information gathered by the Summit County Chapter of the Ohio Genealogical Society to help families find their lost loved ones.

The potter's field is still dear to me, but I don't go as often as I used to. I'm troubled by the unending obscurity the cemetery endures, despite its new position as part of the Metro Parks. Perhaps one day the county will move that massive monument to the entrance, to acknowledge it and focus the community's attention on all those souls. Because even a tale that's mostly fiction is better than no tale at all.

ARCHIE
THE SNOWMAN

By Joanna Wilson

I wasn't having any of it. My mother brought my older sister and me to Chapel Hill Mall each year to visit with Archie the Talking Snowman. But I wasn't fooled. Snowmen don't talk, and I didn't trust the disembodied voice that floated from above. Not even when my older sister enjoyed talking with Archie. Not even for a piece of candy.

Nearly everybody from Akron knows that Archie is a 20-foot-tall snowman that stands in the center of Chapel Hill Mall at Christmastime. He talks to children about their Christmas wishes. Although Archie's eyes are now blue, when I was a child in the 1970s, his eyes were red and the lights inside his eyes flashed when he spoke. The floor-to-ceiling Christmas attraction made me feel wary even if every other child knew Archie was Santa Claus' best friend.

Yeah, I wasn't having any of it.

But tens of thousands of children each year during the 1970s and '80s at Chapel Hill Mall were having it, and loving it. Archie is and was Akron's Christmas celebrity.

Archie looks like your typical three-ball snowman with buttons down his midsection. He wears a scarf and a top hat, and clasps a straw broom in his mittened hand. He is usually surrounded by an elaborate display. The Snow Village—or Archie Land, as people call it – is an arctic vision of pine trees, oversized candy canes, and twinkling lights strung between holiday boughs. Animatronic deer and forest creatures live here, along with Eskimos and their igloos, penguins, smaller snowmen, and elves.

Inside a little cottage in Archie Land, an adult uses a speaker and microphone to talk with children brave enough to step up to the two-story snowman. The person working as the voice of Archie presses a button to light up his eyes as he speaks. This interactive dialogue is Archie's real charm; it's what has made him such a fixture in the lives of generations of Akron children.

Even if I didn't have the fortitude to step up to the wooden platform and speak with Archie when I was a child, I didn't forget about him, either. When I left town for college in the 1980s, I told my new friends about the giant mall snowman from my hometown. In the '90s, "Archie the Talking Snowman" was one of my first image searches on the Internet, in order to verify my childhood

Visit the Talking Snow Man

cb

at Chapel Hill's
Snow Village:
(center court)

**Bring the children!
Our snow man will
talk to them
daily between
4 and 8:30 o'clock.**

Visit every store in the Chapel Hill Shopping Community
Enjoy the comfort of Chapel Hill's covered, completely
air-conditioned Mall for your Christmas shopping.

A&P	Gray Drug Store	New York Bakery	Singer Sewing
Akron National Bank	Holiday Shoes	Nobil Shoes	Spencer Gifts
Andre Duval Beauty Salon	Household Finance	O'Neil's	Stefani's
Baker's Shoes	Koch's	Parklane Hosiery	Tall Styles
Barricini's	Kroger's	Paul Harris	Thom McAn Shoes
Clarkins Optical	Lang's	Penneys	Tie Rak
Cleveland Fabrics	Le Petit Cafe	Petrie's	The Village Store
Cowell & Hubbard	Memory Lane	Pollyanna	Walden's Book Store
Chapel Hill Barber Shop	Metzger's	Record Land	Winkleman's
Cinema I & II	Miller's Jr. Shoe Port	Richman Brothers	Woolworth's
Dixie Hats	Mode O'Day	Rizzi Toys	Zale's
Fuflik Shoes	National Skirt Shop	Sears	
Fanny Farmer Candies			
Flagg Brothers Shoes			
Foxwood Donuts			

ON BUCHHOLZER BLVD *Goodyear Service Store, Goodyear Bank*
ON INDEPENDENCE AVE. *Forest City Interiors*

memories. Leaving Akron made me realize just how much Archie defined Christmas in my hometown.

It turned out I wasn't the only one who thought so. In 2011 Tommy Uplinger returned to Akron after living several years in Florida, and was disappointed to find that Chapel Hill Mall had retired Archie in 2004. Looking to change what he thought was a mistake, Tommy started a Facebook group in November 2011 to try to rally his friends to bring the snowman back. Soon after, Tommy enlisted his friend David Burkett to help him revive their favorite local Christmas attraction for their growing families. Ra'ul Umaña, a former mall employee who worked as the voice of Archie and helped to re-install the snowman and his display in the mall's center court for years, also joined the effort.

What started as a modest campaign, though, clearly struck a nerve: within a few weeks, more than 10,000 people had joined the "Bring Archie Back to Chapel Hill Mall" Facebook group. The earliest discussions in that group included questions about why Chapel Hill Mall had abandoned Archie, where Archie was now, and what could be done to bring Archie back. For some new members, the group was the first news that Archie hadn't been at the mall in seven years. What everyone in the group shared was a strong memory of the talking snowman and a passion for changing the state of things. People began sharing their childhood memories of Archie, Archie's importance to their holiday celebrations, and concerns that the next generation of Akron's children would lack access to a cherished, community holiday tradition. People who had moved away from Akron over the years also found the group, expanding its reach far beyond Akron residents. Hard-to-find photos began surfacing as family after family began uploading old snapshots of children standing in front of the twenty-foot icon during his 36 years of life at the mall.

What happened next surprised everyone. During the first week of December 2011, press releases about the history of Archie the Talking Snowman, his retirement, and the Facebook group of thousands of members went viral. Not only did local journalists pick up the story, but the Associated Press circulated the odd tale about the twenty-foot snowman and his admirers. The story ran around the country.

To the Akronites who wanted to bring Archie back, the snowman was more than just a quirky element of the past that made for an odd news story. Like many Rust Belt cities, Akron had seen decades of decline. Uplinger and his group felt they had endured one too many losses. But here was one piece of Akron culture they thought they could save.

By the middle of 2012, Akron's then-deputy mayor David Lieberth offered Uplinger and his team the opportunity to rebuild the talking snowman at Lock 3, to be a part of the city's annual holiday festivities. Umaña, who had carpentry experience and the background in installing Archie at the mall, was enlisted to lead the reconstruction, and he organized dozens of volunteers to create the surrounding display space called "The Archie Encounter." One year after Tommy's movement began, Archie the Talking Snowman had returned.

And all was right again for Christmastime in Akron.

I was inspired by the compelling story of Archie's return, and decided to write a local history book about it. My research led me to discover much more.

Archie the Talking Snowman's history begins not with his start in 1968 at Chapel Hill Mall but with the start of Christmas attractions developed by downtown retailers as early as the 1910s and '20s. Christmas attractions were created by retailers to lure shoppers to their stores for holiday buying. As crass as it sounds, these attractions, when repeated year after year, often grew to become beloved holiday traditions. As Akron's rubber industry developed during the early part of the twentieth century, the industry's workers provided a stable flow of cash to the city's economy. Downtown retailers such as O'Neil's, Polsky's, and Yeager's competed for shoppers' loyalty, especially during the Christmas boom each year.

In those days, nearly every department store already offered children the opportunity to meet Santa Claus during Christmas. By the 1920s, storefront windows were filled with eye-catching toy displays. In the 1930s the retailers added walk-through attractions to bring shoppers through the doors.

Anchoring the downtown shopping district were the gigantic department stores O'Neil's and Polsky's, which faced each other on Main Street for 50 years. The stores' rivalry peaked each year at Christmastime, when they tried to outdo each other with expressions of holiday splendor. The history of these competitive Christmas displays is dizzying with details of breathtaking sights and what seems like limitless budgets. By mid-century, the competition and escalation in eye-catching holiday attractions between downtown retailers challenged the suburban plaza owners and mall developers to create their own attractions to bring Christmas shoppers to their locations.

To give you an idea of what I mean, here are just a few outstanding examples of the Christmas attractions in Akron over the past one hundred years. In 1917, during World War I, patriotism joined the Christmas spirit at O'Neil's, where children visited Uncle Sam along with Santa Claus. In 1933, O'Neil's offered a walk-through zeppelin "ride" to the North Pole. A giant, metal structure allowed children to walk through the aircraft that featured cabin windows through which they could follow the zeppelin's journey past fairy castles, Eskimo villages, and passing aircraft. Exiting at the other end of the zeppelin, the children arrived at the fairyland of the North Pole, otherwise known as O'Neil's toy department. In a city long known as a research and manufacturing center for airships like blimps and zeppelins, the walk-though zeppelin must have been a can't-miss experience.

O'Neil's followed up that effort in 1934 with Disney-character mechanical figures filling its windows. Inside the store, children were entertained with marionette shows and a Mickey Mouse Castle display.

Holiday-themed puppet shows became so popular that they were staged each year in the storefront windows at both O'Neil's and Polsky's during World War II. Celebrity guests appeared, including beauty pageant winners and local TV kiddie show hosts such as Barnaby, Captain Penny, Franz the Toymaker, Miss Barbara from Romper Room, and even the irreverent horror movie host Ghoulardi. Stores began to kick off the holiday shopping season with such fanfare that the arrival of Santa Claus became a spectacle not to be missed. Would you believe that St. Nick arrived downtown by helicopter in 1954, riding a space satellite up Main Street in 1957, driving a Conestoga wagon in 1959, and seated atop a live elephant at Chapel Hill Mall in 1967? Both Polsky's and O'Neil's established traditions of Nativity displays to appeal to those interested in the more sacred and reverent sentiments of the holiday season, too.

And Archie the Snowman was not the only talking Christmas attraction in Akron. There were at least six other talking Christmas figures over the decades. Polsky's department store trotted out Tom the Talking Horse throughout the 1940s. A more traditional Rudolph the Red-Nosed Reindeer replaced him for a few years in the early 1950s, until the very popular Tom made a comeback. Across Main Street, O'Neil's eventually followed suit in 1965, with a talking Christmas tree. These Christmas characters so solidified their place in Akron tradition that any new mall felt obliged to compete. Chapel Hill Mall opened in 1966, and in 1968 brought Archie to life. Summit Mall offered its own competitor the same year, a talking Christmas tree in its center court. In 1972, O'Neil's upgraded its talking tree to a more unique giant Raggedy Ann doll.

A few years later, Akron's third mall, Rolling Acres, created a fifteen-foot-tall talking giant named RA (pronounced "Ray") as the personification of the mall's new logo. This weird plethora begs the question—what giant Christmas object were Akron's children NOT talking with?

All of these talking attractions were brought out for at least several Christmas seasons; Archie, however, lasted the longest. He was a popular feature at Chapel Hill Mall for thirty-six holidays, from 1968-2003. His retirement was due, at least in part, to the mall's new out-of-state owners' desire to update by moving away from using an old-fashioned promotion each holiday season.

Another reason for the retirement—and not a small one—was the fact that consumer habits changed between 1968 and the beginning of the 21st century. The rubber industry that fueled downtown retail competition and much of the city's economy was decimated. Not only had rubber fled, but residents no longer shopped downtown, preferring to spend their money at area plazas and malls. In the 1960s, Yeager's closed after 55 years of business downtown. O'Neil's and Polsky's had ended their elaborate Christmas attractions and shuttered their doors completely by the end of the 1980s. By the 2000s, Christmas attractions were gone from the city because shoppers were buying more and more online, and looking for deep discounts at Black Friday sales rather than seeking entertainment during the holidays. Archie seemed a relic of the past.

Fortunately, like any classic Christmas tale, this one has a happy ending. After two years at Lock 3, Archie was reinstalled at Chapel Hill Mall in 2014, much to the delight of the new mall management company and Akron residents.

Archie the Talking Snowman was and is special because he isn't concerned with judging naughty or nice but welcomes all for a pleasant conversation. Archie doesn't usually ask what children want for Christmas—that's Santa's job. He's more concerned with how children feel, the friends and family they are shopping for, and offering them an opportunity to express their holiday joy.

But children aren't Archie's biggest fans; rather, it's the adults who grew up with him as a Christmas tradition who want to share

Archie with their own children and grandchildren. Archie's biggest supporters have been the adults who built him, worked as his voice over the years, and petitioned for his return after he was retired.

Spending time at the mall during the holiday season in 2015 gave me the opportunity to watch as children continue to enact the decades-long tradition of speaking with Archie the Talking Snowman. Even if adults look at Archie and see an imperfectly handmade, dusty snowman that everyone cynically swears was much taller when they were children, I can attest that today's youth still see Archie with the same excitement and magic that originally drew us all in. Standing next to Archie Land, you can watch youngsters approach the microphone, wide-eyed. Many children are overwhelmed with excitement as they wait in line or rattle off a long list of things they want Archie to tell Santa they want for Christmas. One child I saw this past year stepped up to the microphone and simply screamed. It was a sustained howl that lasted long enough to frighten every shopper and store employee at the one end of the mall – all of us looking around for the person who must be dying. But we all began gently giggling once we laid eyes on the toddler, standing in front of Archie, expressing his Christmas joy at the top of his lungs. On another day at the mall, I overheard Archie respond to a child, "You'll shoot your eye out, kid." Immediately recognizing the line as a quote from the 1983 movie *A Christmas Story*, I looked over to see the eight-year-old boy at the microphone laughing and grabbing at his little brother, while a parent nearby also chuckled. Archie continued, "What do you want with a BB gun?" and without hearing the child's half of the conversation, all the on-lookers were in on the joke too.

Archie continues to be important to me because I see that this story is very much an Akron story. Although internet shopping may have made retail Christmas attractions like Archie seem obsolete, it is also the Internet and the successful use of social media that brought our city's favorite holiday tradition back to life. Archie is Akron, as we all continue to persevere and redefine ourselves in the ever-changing world while holding traditions close to our hearts. Even if I wasn't open to Archie as a child, I feel like we've grown to be very good friends now.

MAJOR STEPS

By Rita Dove

Originally published July 10, 2005, in the Washington Post.
Reprinted by permission of Rita Dove.

"You can always get warm, but it's hard to stay cool." My mother's words, muttered every summer since I can remember, rang like a mantra in my head as I stood in the uncut grass of a football field (the 20-yard line, to be precise), knees locked and eyes forward, arms akimbo, to balance a 28-inch-long metal stick at a 45-degree angle, just so. Perspiration trickled down my temples and collected under my jaw, but I held still. Since reaching my teens, I'd come to dread the wasteland of summer vacation—heat and more heat, the sodden press of humidity that could force my painfully coiffed pageboy to retract its hooks, sun that turned my caramel complexion to burnt umber if I forgot to wear a hat.

It was the 19th of August, 1968, four days until the Soap Box Derby Parade and nine days before my sixteenth birthday, and I still hadn't figured out how to keep my minimalist emergency 'do (French twist with bangs pinned to the side) from shrinking to that fine corona of frizz usually found in the *National Geographic* photographs of ostrich heads. Why, oh why was I standing here at attention like a tin soldier, ankle-deep in crabgrass in the middle of a sweltering Midwestern summer, sweating out all the good sense Mom had pressed into the curls on my head?

Four months earlier, in April, a week or so after Martin Luther King Jr.'s murder, I was packing up my cello one afternoon after orchestra practice when Rhonda bounded up, flute propped on her shoulder like a baseball bat, and clapped me on the back. Rhonda was always doing things like that; copper-skinned and confident (even in glasses!) to the point of being uncomfortably gung-ho, she was what my grandmother would call, wrinkling her nose, sturdy. I started to straighten up, but she couldn't wait. "Rita," she whispered, "I've got a terrific idea. Let's try out for the majorette squad!"

Funny thing is, even though I gulped and felt my heart pound into my throat, I thought it was a great idea, too. In the Byzantine hierarchy of high school, majorettes and cheerleaders were the Cream. Cheerleaders enjoyed a noisy devotion from the masses, but majorettes were the serene wizards, the silvery circumferences of their batons humming before them like horizontal pirouettes. If I said yes, if I tried out and actually made the squad, maybe I could finally be . . . I closed my eyes to savor the possibility—popular. Just thinking the word sent a shiver of longing through me. What was it like? Ever since junior high, I'd been called "brainiac." I thought I was used to it, but sometimes, on pale-green spring mornings or glimpsing the tentative expression on my face reflected in a store window, I'd wonder. Although I'd never been exactly reviled, had never borne the brunt of schoolyard taunts or classroom pranks, I'd also never been pursued by a boy, at least not ardently. I could not imagine attaining the courtly cool of Carla, every hair in perfect alignment against her cocoa profile. Nor could I ever hope for the effervescent cuteness of Quinita, barely five feet tall, with wide-spaced, tilted almond eyes large enough to bring any basketball player down to her size. I just wanted . . . well, not to be regarded with dread or, worse, utter indifference. But how to accomplish that, skinny-Minnie me with my Catwoman glasses and hair that frizzled in the rain because I was not allowed to put a relaxer in it? How could someone who attended all AP classes and played cello in the school orchestra become popular?

I picked up my bow from the music stand and loosened it, slowly. "Why not?" I replied, utterly cool.

We figured the only way to break the barrier of the all-white majorette squad was to make it impossibly hard for them to refuse us. Rhonda had taken twirling lessons before and volunteered to coach me during the open training session offered by the senior majorettes during the last weeks of the school year.

We joined the other supplicants after school in the incandescent gloom of the band room for a crash course in twirls—verticals and frontals, figure eights, around the worlds—which Rhonda supplemented later in her basement, enthusiastically breaking down each sleight of hand into its elemental actions: wrist down then wrist up, clockwise then counter.

For the second week, we broke into groups to learn a routine of our choice, which we were expected to perform for auditions that Friday. Rhonda made for Donna's corner. I followed, reluctantly; Donna was a senior and the best twirler on the team, and I found the gleaming blond waves capping her stocky frame rather frightening. But when she announced, "This routine is hard, you'll have to work," looking each of us in the eye without much hope or even sympathy, I began to like her: Fair was fair. By audition time, I knew the routine as well as Rhonda; we had even invented a few moves of our own. We were careful not to show our cards, though; we never stood next to each other during practice or laughed at each other's jokes. An old survival trick: Don't give them a chance to cry disrespect. If they're going to dismiss you, at least make them scramble for their excuses.

And so it happened that in Akron, Ohio, for the 1968-69 school year, two Negroes joined the Buchtel High School majorettes: a Historic First. The neighborhood buzzed, my mother beamed, the president of the local NAACP chapter came up after church to shake my hand. Even my father, usually dismissive of nonintellectual pursuits, pulled out his camera as I struck a few poses in the driveway.

The first item on the outgoing majorettes' agenda was to form the new Line. We were ranked by height, then shuffled among the returning twirlers with adjustments for body build, hair color and style—and complexion. No one mentioned race, but it was on everyone's mind that year, and it hung in the meeting room until Rhonda blurted out: "What are we, a handful of M&M's?" We all laughed, and that was that. There were too many other things demanding our attention: marching techniques and stand-alone routines, halftime formations and pep rally drills. We practiced every afternoon after school in the deserted hallways. The seniors stood apart, arms crossed, forbearing and aloof. Beth, Cindy, Toni: veterans on the Line, proprietors of all Knowledge, purveyors of Secret Remedies (Vaseline on bare legs in winter, Band-Aids on heels to prevent blisters), our shepherds through the Valley of the Shadow of Football Seasons Past. It was heady but confusing: flash a smile but maintain synchronicity, switch your hips while lifting your knees, high step and sashay. The amount of paraphernalia was staggering–two uniforms (cotton for summer parades, corduroy for the fall), regulation boots with pom-poms, kid gloves for November games. When Donna offered to sell me her gear, I hesitated, sniffing condescension (All Blacks are poor, live in the ghetto, etc.), until she pointed out that we were about the same height and it was silly to waste money on a vaguely militaristic outfit I'd wear for four months out of the year. So I walked with her to the white neighborhood two blocks the other way from school and sat on a chenille bedspread eerily similar to my own as she rummaged through her closet. Two grocery bags full. She even threw in the corduroy underwear.

"Hey, you finally got one!" I ducked my head to hide my irritation, but the pigtailed little girl squatting in the grass would not be deterred. "That's good!" she said. "Aren't you glad?" I stole a glance at Rhonda throwing aerials at the far end of the yard to the oohs and aahs of a pack of neighborhood kids. Big deal. After snatching at air for a half-hour, it was about time I caught the thing.

My champion twitched her fat braids—now she was irritated, too—and called out, "Hey, she caught it!"

Rhonda trotted over. "I told you it'd work itself out! You just have to plug away until your arm remembers by itself!"

Rhonda was the technique guru, while I thrived on artistic expression; we pushed each other. Every weekend that spring found us in my side yard, polishing the routines and trying out new tricks. The secret to retrieving a baton tossed into the air—as I was to learn that afternoon of miss upon near-miss, the kids squealing in delight as they rippled to a safe orbit—is not to try too hard to catch it. Once you send the baton spinning skyward, calmly released from the upturned palm, all you have to do is wait, gauging the instant when it will return to waist level, then reach and pluck it out of the air, like a flower. Easy enough, once you know.

The school year ended in the usual flurry of exams and social events; band and majorette practice would resume three weeks before Derby Day in August, when kids from all over the world descended upon Akron to race their motorless wooden cars in the All-American Soap Box Derby. I took a vacation from twirling to spend a few weeks curled on the couch reading before growing restless – in the wake of Bobby Kennedy's assassination, with the accelerating madness of Vietnam in plain television view, it seemed the entire country was growing more and more restless. But while the streets seethed with angry, disheartened protesters, I checked out library books on Eastern philosophies and sat cross-legged on the floor of my room, shades drawn and incense burning, hip sockets screeching in agony as I intoned "om" to a recording of Buddhist monks. Nirvana escaped me, but it didn't matter: August neared, with the promise of being allowed onto our Half-Time Stage: the Gridiron.

Beth's whistle pumped out the beat: 1, 2, 3, 4. Hard to stay cool, indeed: I was delirious with heat, my temples throbbing in march tempo while we advanced on burning feet up the ragged field, my fingers thick and slick as sausages–which meant slippage, a slower baton, more wrist action, more effort, more sweat. Wait till winter, the freshly risen seniors warned with a chuckle, it'll freeze to your fingers. Then try catching an aerial! They loved scaring us, it was part of the ritual. Rhonda and I vowed we would show them.

Right now, though, this slithery silver wand was not behaving. I cast a surreptitious look down the Line: Ruthie, shortest and terminally cute, was the veteran among us juniors, having already marched in her sophomore year. Elaine's brown hair curled gently around her roses-and-cream complexion; she constantly had to be told not to slump. Jackie was tall, too, and dark in a Mediterranean way, with a nose that jutted out like Cher's—Rhonda and I agreed it looked sexy.

Caught up in my own deficiencies, I couldn't understand that each girl had her secret shortcomings–Jackie wanted Ruthie's pert nose, Ruthie covertly envied Beth's narrow one; Cindy deplored her skinny legs, which Elaine coveted. Christine despaired over her hair, fine and blond, which she claimed was unmanageable. How could I ever fit into this group that laughed so easily and seemed not to mind the heat? But it was more than that: they possessed the power of assumption; they'd grown up assuming the world was theirs to grow up into. Every little detail of their daily lives–flesh-toned Band-Aids and nude-colored brassieres, the shades of face powder available at Woolworth's cosmetic counter and, yes, the hair products lining the shelves–was buoyed by the mainstream they floated in.

As we ran through the roster for Derby Day (which would be our first gig, replete with real celebrities—Trini Lopez!—in the grandstand and tens of thousands of spectators), the seniors doled out anecdotes and advice in equally sadistic measures. Take salt tablets to counteract the fluids you lose, so you don't faint. Sweat? You haven't seen sweat yet . . . it'll blind you, pool in your boots. Apropos boots—wear at least two pairs of bobby socks. Better your feet burn up than getting blisters! You'll forget your feet, anyway—too much noise and bright lights. Then, after you've marched past Polsky's department store, after you can't hear the horns anymore because those guys' lips are blown and all you can do is try to find the bass drum beat in that racket (refrain from licking your sweat, let it drip gracefully) . . . after you've given up trying to smile at the crowds lining the curb and you just want to sit down and pull off those ridiculous pom-pommed boots that weigh a ton by now and make you feel like a Clydesdale while looking like a Lipizzaner—then comes Derby Hill.

Oh, it's a mean hill, they exclaimed, steep and single-minded! You march your weary thighs to the starting line, wait for the trumpet fanfare, then step over the precipice. Pure perpendicular, braking with your heels, your calf muscles screaming as they contract. You don't know pain until you do the Hill.

"C'mon, Rita, it's easy!" Jackie pushed her way through the gaggle of girls, her smooth, locket-shaped face thrust forward, laughing. Now the world would know. Come one, come all: behold the asphalt flower in her reinforced tennis shoes!

I scanned the circle: barefoot, every one of them. How could these white girls have this over me, too? Every summer I tried, but my tender soles kept me from going any farther than our gravel driveway. Wasn't I supposed to have come from the jungle to these shores, in chains and certainly barefoot? What had happened to my gene pool?

"It's all grass. Padded—just like your carpet at home!"

Who said that? Had to be a senior. I peered over Jackie's shoulder and caught sight of Rhonda, hanging back at the fringe, grinning.

"You'll be much cooler. And you won't run a blister," said Christine, whose nose was beginning to peel despite the floppy cotton hat she'd screwed on over her limp hair.

It was the perspiration sheen across Christine's cheeks that convinced me. If she could suffer, so could I. I wriggled out of my sneakers, wavered on damp, puckery feet. Hoots and whistles, Rhonda's clomping applause. We fell in at the 50-yard line and waited for the whistle's count before peeling into the "Colonel Bogey March," with its easy reverse vertical twirls low to one side, then the swooping back-bending strut that looked so hard but was breezingly simple—perfect for the end of a long parade and the approach to Derby Hill, where leaning backward would counterbalance the pitch of the racetrack slope.

The grass was cool, the ground deliciously warm underneath. After a few measures I got used to the feathery pokes between my toes, an occasional flicker tickling my ankles. My knees snapped to my chest as I high-stepped, switching my hips. How tantalizing it was after all these years, to feel the earth under the soft skin of my feet!

Then I stopped mid-step, howling: A pain suffused me, immediate and pure, almost sweet in its ferocity. It seemed to shoot out of the earth, straight up from Hell's flame pits. I dropped and rolled, clutching my right foot. Instinct, it seemed, knew right away where it hurt, while my overactive brain went nova. Jackie was the first one over, but Elaine made the pronouncement: "You've been stung!" She gently unfolded my clenched toes to expose the dull red stinger, still lodged in the crevice of my little toe. Stung? By what? I was incredulous. A bee sting hurts this much? Somewhere behind the throbbing and a sympathetic headache, I was ashamed of my ignorance. Ruthie ran for the first-aid kit and pulled the stinger out.

I insisted on walking the few blocks home. When I stumbled into the kitchen, Mom lit into action, popping ice cubes into a pail of water. My brother, dangerously allergic to bee stings, took one look, panicked, and began pacing, so Mom sent him upstairs for iodine just as 10-year-old Robin, sensing family drama, rushed in from play. "Ooh, that's nasty!" she shrieked, plainly delighted. "How ya gonna march now?"

Although Mom applied crushed aspirin directly to the puncture, by dinnertime not even a sandal fit over my swollen foot. Yet I remained calm. One thing was certain: I would march on Derby Day, even if I had to hop on one boot.

I spent the next day on the couch, foot propped up, but demanded to attend practice the last afternoon before the parade. Mom dropped me off at the edge of the field and I limped to the bleachers to watch. That night, a dry run with gauze and one sock instead of two: Tears shot into my eyes when we maneuvered the boot on. By the time we'd jimmied it off and I had taken my clump foot and ice pack to bed, I was too wrung out to despair.

Derby Day dawned clear and hot. By rush hour, downtown was thick with enflamed smog from the tire factories. Stir in the kind of mugginess the Midwest does best, and by seven in the evening we'd be slogging through warm pudding.

A funny thing: Pain endured in service of desire, even one as trivial as marching in a parade, doesn't stay still. It may hide a bit at first so you think you've got the upper hand, but then it crescendos—threatening, testing. And if you don't panic, if you accept and even invite that pain to become a part of yourself (I thought of the Buddhist monks and chanted silently with them), then you can turn the corner and go on forever. I remember every minute of that parade—the grit flying in our faces when we turned off Main Street, the weird way buildings amplified or swallowed the music, how I quenched my thirst with my own sweat and how the taste changed from salty to bitter, the wink Rhonda threw me in the middle of our high school's fight song, just before the right turn. And there it was: the Hill.

We paused on the crest, hands on our hips in identical chevrons, our black-and-white uniforms looking crisp despite the heat. A faint wind teased, a cool sigh sweeping up the torched asphalt; at the bottom of the incline autumn waited with the promise of football sweaters, frosty nights and hot chocolate. Suddenly Beth's whistle blew, more a shriek than a call to arms; the band lurched into the perky opening measures of the "Colonel Bogey March," and we stepped off.

Why did marching down the Hill feel so good that August evening? It was the last hurdle, of course, in a transition I had hoped to negotiate with some measure of grace. But it was more physical and metaphysical than that. As the ground under my feet gave way, I trusted the laws of gravity and physics, and they did not let me down; instead, I lay back, and they held me on a cushion of air plumped by the throbbing of the band behind me, pulsing in time with my swollen toe way down there nestled in gauze and one cotton sock, safe in my spanking-white boot. The Hill was beneath me and we were all moving down at the same time, the I gloriously aware that as long as she was part of the We there would be no slipping—just lay back and let the ground tug you along.

And in that instant of buoyant locomotion I knew, suddenly and very clearly, that being a majorette wasn't going to make me popular. Maybe even the opposite—boys would be scared of Little Miss Overachiever more than ever. I no longer cared. I'd be sunburnt red as a brick, wind-chapped and rusty-shinned, and oh, what a mess my hair would be, but it all would be over too soon, like the summer I'd left at the top of the hill.

BUTTS UP

By Mike Gruss

I cradled my head in my arms, ducked against the three-story brick wall and waited.

About 15 middle school boys stood a free-throw's distance behind me—my back, ass and legs a target for these newly-minted teenagers armed with a tennis ball.

The hurt would come.

Humiliation and pain are a regular part of many 13-year-old's lives. This particular instance in my upbringing was the punishing part of a game we called Butts Up. Butts Up dominated every seventh and eighth grade boy's recess in 1990 at the small school I attended in Bath, Ohio, a tony rural suburb about 20 miles northwest of Akron. For my peer group, it was a kind of social phenomenon. Everyone played. To sit out was unthinkable.

I spent hours learning how to master the finer points, how to improve my hand-eye coordination, and how to survive. In short, I spent hours trying to figure out what all kids that age do: how to avoid the brutal worst-case scenario.

In Butts Up, the worst case was known as a royal, a time when every player lined up and, one by one, took unobstructed shots at a classmate's behind.

I bent over.

From under my arms, I could hear the woosh of the tennis ball as it rushed toward me, the thud of it against my skin, the involuntary grunt once my nerves processed what had happened. Woosh. Thud. Oof.

The first ball arrived on the curve of my back. Then another. Then another.

Butts Up was as much a part of my eighth-grade year as the blue and khaki colors required in the dress code or the theatrical production of *Oliver!* Butts Up was like a bad girlfriend – an important part of my life for an intense but brief period and then never heard from again.

Today's middle-schoolers have grown up when dodge ball and tackle football are all but extinct at recess. But for those of us at Old Trail in the late 1980s and early 1990s, we had Butts Up, and we endured its repetition as part of our education.

Woosh. Thud. Oof. Woosh. Thud. Oof.

A direct hit would be felt deep in the quads, in the ass, in the calves, in the back, and yes, if a player didn't stand quite right, in the balls. That's exactly where 13-year-old boys aim.

Oof.

The rules of Butts Up seemed simple enough. The first player threw a tennis ball against the wall. The other players tried to catch it, and then took their own turns, throwing it back against the wall. If they missed or fumbled the ball though, they had to immediately run to the wall and touch it before another player hit them with the ball.

And that is where it got tricky.

If you were struck on the way to the wall, the person who nailed you got to take another, free shot at you with the tennis ball. You got a lesson in taking your lumps.

If you moved out of the way during this free shot or did anything to avoid the pain that was due, you opened yourself up to a whole new hell: a royal.

Then, every player could take a shot at you, one at a time. This process seemingly could take much of recess.

Once you survived this firing range, you had to run past a certain point on the blacktop, in this case an imaginary line extending from a tree, dodging one final throw. If you were hit, then you went through the whole exercise of taking a shot again.

The equipment was spare: a tennis ball and a brick wall. At Old Trail, the wall was a barn-sized canvas, encompassing a classroom on the first floor, the science lab above it and the art room one story up. The tennis ball always seemed to magically appear.

Butts Up was a remarkable display of minimalism at a private school that had everything. Located in the Cuyahoga Valley National Park, Old Trail has been home to a who's who of Akron names. The children of a Cavs player and Browns coach attended the school. The owners of national retail chains sent their offspring there. So did lawyers, doctors, and executive-suite business-types. Since I graduated, in 1991, the school has taken on a greater focus on sustainability and environmentalism. But the core message has stayed the same: personalized, compassionate, enlightened education (kindergartners took French).

During an English class my eighth grade year, we read *Lord of the Flies*, the story of marooned teenage boys sorting themselves into a social hierarchy and trying to survive any way they can.

On the playground, we lived it.

No one at Old Trail remembers exactly when the game started surfacing at recess, but the conventional wisdom says a student from Brecksville introduced it in the mid-1980s. From then on, Butts Up was passed along from one year's students to the next.

As an adult, my former fascination with the game is inexplicable, one of a series of bad choices adolescent minds make, almost like working a terrible job or liking a lame band and then years later wondering, why was I into that? Why did I let that happen as long as it did?

Why did I play? I don't know. I just … did.

When did I realize this was not the typical game middle school boys play? I don't know. High school? College? Maybe I knew at the time? As a Boy Scout at nearby Camp Manatoc, my friends and I held "Wedgie Wars," where we would stand on bunk beds, joust for position, and try to rip each other's tighty-whitey underwear by giving the opponent massive wedgies. We would tie each other to posts to practice knots or light tennis balls on fire. We spent hours playing the chase-and-tackle game with the outdated and now-embarrassing name "smear the queer." We were, to rationalize it in a word, boys. Butts Up, for all its odd rituals, was within the realm of normal behavior.

Still, too often when adults look back on their so-called formative teenage years, we look at what happened with a particular teacher or coach or moment in the classroom or at a school dance or during a sleepover or on the class trip to Toronto where the boys weren't supposed to have adjoining hotel rooms with the girls but somehow they did. But rarely do we think about what happened on the playground and how it shaped us, because recess, we are told, over and over again while we are in school, is insignificant.

Until, of course, it's not.

Butts Up was not limited to Old Trail in the 1990s. According to online accounts, its roots date back to the 1940s or 1950s. In the 2008 book, *Children's Folklore: A Handbook*, by Elizabeth Tucker, students in Utah said they took part in a game called Butts Up in the 1980s.

"Playground supervisors discouraged them from playing it," the book observed.

In other parts of the country, the game was known as Bootie's Up, Bootie's Ball, Wall Ball, and Spread.

I had never heard of any of them when, in the fall of 1990, I transferred to Old Trail from a much larger junior high in Hudson, another Akron suburb. Old Trail was my third school in three years and, while I didn't know it at the time, the middle of a string of five schools over five years as my parents divorced and settled into new lives.

With the knowledge of 25 years of hindsight, I guess my seventh grade year had been a disappointment academically and socially. I underperformed in many classes—forgetting to do key assignments and struggling to grasp pre-algebra—and didn't make many new friends.

Old Trail was small, just 35 students in my grade, and my mother worked as the secretary for the headmaster. It gave me a fresh start.

On the first day of school, there was no other option for recess for boys. To be accepted, to join a peer group as the new kid, meant to play Butts Up.

At first the game seemed fast. Foreign. It was not football, with its universal rules and playground tweaks or chatting on the swings. A few years earlier, I had joined a Battle of the Books team, which involved reading and answering trivia questions, as a way to meet my classmates. It was every bit as nerdy as it sounds.

Butts Up was pretty much the exact opposite of that.

Within weeks of my arrival, I found my comfort zone. In the classroom, I continued to sweat too much, talk too much, make jokes that weren't funny. But I settled in and eventually made friends. I slow-danced to Extreme at mixers and played goalie on the second-string soccer team. In the school musical, I portrayed the Artful Dodger. My grades improved significantly from the year before.

At recess, I played Butts Up.

When I've talked about the game as an adult, my friends, particularly women, have asked how I functioned the rest of the school day. Did I dread playing? Was I relieved when it was over? Did I foam at the mouth like the rabid animals I was emulating every afternoon? Had I sweated through my clothes? Did I emit a teenage locker room funk the rest of the day? Was I distracted from the stain a muddy tennis ball left on my khakis?

I don't know. There are no scars—physical or emotional—to remind me.

In some parts of the country, kids played a variation of Butts Up that produced a champion. Not at Old Trail. Our version was an endless run of throws and misses and tortures, starting when students stepped onto the blacktop in fifth or sixth grade and continuing until we graduated from middle school. It was workmanlike, preparing us to clock in and clock out for our jobs in ten years, an early lesson in the repetitive monotony of life.

I don't remember playing anything but Butts Up at recess my eighth-grade year. The younger students had yet to be exposed. I have no idea where the girls in my class went. Maybe they walked the campus? Maybe they chatted on the swings about what savages we were? Even on days when it rained or snowed, I think we moved the game indoors to the gym – same tennis ball, different brick wall.

And to what end?

In traditional sports, players are conditioned to gain something from the exercise. The clichés are endless: athletes learned to push themselves to the limit, they learned the value of teamwork, they learned to keep a loss in perspective. Blah-blah-blah.

But what—if anything—can be learned from a game that requires middle school boys to bend over and take it?

I tracked down several former classmates to talk about our long-ago collective obsession. I have spent my professional life working as a reporter, calling strangers and cajoling them to explain education policies and state politics and defense spending bills to me. Yet it was a special kind of anxiety to dial my former classmates, some of whom I hadn't spoken to in 20 years, and ask about all those times they got pegged in the ass with a tennis ball.

My fears were unfounded. Their memories were vivid. No one remembered a particularly dominating player (although plenty of embarrassing ones), an especially gruesome welt, an amazing feat of athleticism. There was no epic, unforgettable game.

What they did remember, once the fog of memory cleared, was the strategy, a player taxonomy that forced us to play to our strengths.

The kids who were fastest often hovered closest to the wall, believing that if they were to fumble the ball they were quick enough to save themselves without getting hit. The downside? They faced the most chances of getting pegged.

On the other hand, the kids who had the best arms played in the back. Their chances of making a play were fewer and farther between, but they could pick up a ball on a ricochet and nail someone on the way to the wall, an odd badge of honor in the game.

That's where you'd find me. In eighth grade, I envisioned myself as a budding third baseman, capable of snagging a grounder down the line and making the long throw to first. I was beginning to realize that I couldn't hit a fastball, much less a curveball, and, in less than two years, I would fail to make a junior varsity baseball team. But at this age, I still possessed a watered-down version of big-league dreams and stationed myself in the back.

The kids who weren't the fastest or who didn't have the best arms filtered throughout the middle of playing area. The game provided a social order.

My brother, who is five years younger and also went to Old Trail, said he prided himself on taking the shot when it was his turn. Even after the most gruesome hits, he remembered turning to his antagonist and asking, "Is that all you got?" He learned to keep his emotions at bay.

Another classmate acknowledged that the game taught him the value of blending in, of not being the center of attention and, inadvertently thus not becoming the victim of tennis ball beatings. In a weird way, Butts Up, he said, helped him become more even keeled.

I found a certain beauty to the rhythms of the game.

At times, from the back corner, I would nail a classmate on the way to the wall. On the best days, my target was the kind of eighth-grader who gives the new kid shit and who deserves a tennis ball in the tender derriere. Butts Up was a chance at revenge.

At times, I blended in and avoided drawing attention to myself and a bully's gaze. Butts Up was a chance at anonymity.

At times, from the back corner, I could seamlessly pick up the ball and throw it against the wall, keeping the game going. Butts Up was a chance to fit in.

Michael Duff was the head of Old Trail's middle school, and therefore the primary disciplinarian, beginning eight years before I arrived and continuing until his retirement in the spring of 2014.

Butts Up, he said, was "the poster child for what could go wrong" at recess. He called it cruel and said he confiscated more tennis balls over the years than he can remember.

When boys are 12, 13, 14 years old, he told me in an interview, they need to stop having physical interactions with their peers and instead start working on more cerebral relationships, the kind they would have as adults and in high school.

To him, Butts Up was a game where alpha males could dominate and unfairly exert their advantage.

"Most kids in the middle school are looking for a foothold of acceptance," he said. But often the kids that were least apt at the social interactions necessary for middle school, are also the kids least apt at throwing a tennis ball.

Butts Up could be viewed as a rite of passage, but it also could be seen as a type of fraternity hazing. On top of that, the game often excluded girls, which Duff viewed as unhealthy.

Even more intriguing, the game had a history I had never heard about.

Years after my graduation, the school's faculty members, who often monitored students during the games, petitioned successfully to end recess and subsequently their recess duty. One of the major reasons? Butts Up. Male teachers had no problem with the game, but female teachers abhorred it.

By the time recess returned, Butts Up had faded away. No generation to teach the next. A memory.

At my eighth-grade graduation ceremony, where boys often knotted their own long ties for the first time and girls donned white dresses, I won something called the headmaster's spirit award. Typically, it had been recognition for a kid who was not the smartest or most athletic but who had an attitude the school leaders liked.

In short, it was a formal nod of acceptance.

But, in reality, that acknowledgement had come months earlier, on a day on that blacktop.

I had cradled my head in my arms, ducked against the three-story brick wall and waited.

Woosh. Thud. Oof.

I had been hit several times as part of a royal, and the next student to throw was a strong athlete. His blond hair swooped over part of his glasses, possibly, if I was lucky, obscuring his vision. We didn't know each other well and didn't talk much.

I looked back. With all the mechanics of a pitcher throwing a changeup, he released the ball, ever so lightly.

I braced.

No woosh. No thud. No oof. Just a nick, as if the ball had tried to sit on my back, then fallen to the pavement.

But why?

It was one harmless toss in the grand scheme of the year-long game, yet it demonstrated a lesson that eighth-grade boys and plenty of adults struggle to absorb:

Sometimes, you get the privilege of holding the tennis ball and taking aim, ready to prove who's the man and how much pain you can cause. But, just as often, you're on the other end – the one who's vulnerable, cowering with your head in your arms and ducking against a brick wall.

Why has Butts Up stuck with me all these years?

That cruel game taught mercy.

You'll Find It Off Market Street

By Eric Wasserman

It was supposed to be temporary. Just a nice, one-year stint in the Midwest that would lead to a potential opportunity that would return me to the West Coast with more experience and the prospect of better job security. Perhaps getting a full-time teaching position at a good community college.

That was nine years ago.

My wife, Thea, and I had packed up our belongings and pets, took one last glance at the Pacific Ocean and drove my 1996 Chevy Blazer from Santa Monica, California to Akron, Ohio. I seemed to recall from high school learning that there was a big lake near where we would be relocating. The truck was in perfect working order at the time, but the hope was to get my professional life in working order.

The Blazer literally started breaking down the moment we arrived in Akron, just as my career began to soar. I remember asking one of my new colleagues where to go for vehicle service. I was told that the place was "off Market Street." Seriously, it seemed every response to where I should go for anything in Akron was that it was "off Market Street," the main artery that ran through town. Our bank, the dry cleaners, our optometrist, where we bought our groceries, the movie theater up the street from our first apartment, the local coffee shop, The University of Akron that had just hired me for a temporary, one-year visiting assistant professor gig. So, "off Market Street" is where I met my service guru, Tim. Some people think it's important to find a loyal and trustworthy doctor. Tim was my Blazer's version of that. I couldn't have imagined at the time that I would be following him wherever he went (four employment locations in all in just under a decade). I have a service invoice from around that first time we met for a bill of $557.00 for repair work I can't even understand. So much for a privileged graduate school education.

The first thing I noticed about driving in Akron was that the locals apparently viewed using turn signals as merely a suggestion, and the police didn't seem to care. In my first month in Akron I was nearly hit by merging cars on Market Street, which only has two lanes on each side, far more times than in all my previous years driving the seven-plus lanes on each side of the 405 freeway in Los Angeles every day.

But stop signs were another story in Akron. In that first month I rolled a stop in a residential area on a sleepy early September afternoon only to be pulled over and have an officer immediately say to me as I cracked my then still-operating driver's side window, "Where do you think you are, California?" I had actually just gotten my Ohio plates and driver's license a few days before. Unlike Los Angeles though, the officer glanced over the Blazer and said, "Nice ride, used to have one myself. A ninety-six, right?" I was let off with a warning.

The Blazer made it through what was supposed to be just that single year in Akron with Tim performing occasional maintenance that didn't exactly bust my wallet. Then the unthinkable: a last minute tenure-line position came through and I got it. We were staying in Akron. And that's when the Blazer's major problems really began. I have multiple service invoices from around then. Looks like I had to replace the alternator and something labeled "B-GENER REM," whatever the hell that is, for $450.27 (disclaimer: to this day I also have absolutely no idea what the alternator actually is or does).

Unlike that cop who pulled me over, lots of people made fun of my Blazer. I never cared. I once had to meet my cousin's husband at his place of business in Beverly Hills. He had reserved a space for me in his company's parking deck. When I pulled up to the gate the attendant looked at the Blazer like I had brought an ugly date to a high school dance. Not so in Akron. I never got so much street cred in my life than having that American-made Blazer in Northeast Ohio. Akron is, after all, the once great tire-producing mecca. It took a lot for the not-so-nice Jewish boy in me to hide the fact that I don't know a thing about cars other than how to put gas in them, drive them, and throw down my credit cards for repairs. Midwest car people kept telling me 1996 was a great year for Chevy engines, that I was lucky to have my Blazer, that it would probably run forever if I took good care of it. Twice I had complete strangers approach me offering to buy it just for the parts. Contractors who came to work on the century-old house Thea and I bought always complimented the Blazer. I felt like a fraud, but a proud fraud.

Here's the thing, I never expected us to stay in Akron. Even after I was awarded tenure I thought we would be returning to the West Coast at some point. We had made great friends in Akron, had a community, but I just hadn't thought it was permanent. Thea had grown up outside Louisville, Kentucky, so there wasn't too much necessary adjustment to Midwest living on her part. Not so for me.

So, recognizing that there were thousands of academics out there that would die to have my job and I was being kind of an ingrate, I started trying to make Akron my place. I finally signed up for an *Akron Beacon Journal* subscription. I began rooting for the Indians (sorry, I just couldn't bring myself to be a Cavs fan even though LeBron James went to high school down the street). I joined the board of trustees for the local art house cinema. Thea and I started exploring places to make Akron our place (the Towpath Trail of Summit Metro Parks and Cuyahoga Valley National Park quickly became some of my favorite Akron treasures).

Let me tell you though, if anyone asks me to describe Akron locals, the very first thing I say is that, even with their healthy skepticism of outsiders, they want you to love their town, and they welcome you with open arms to experience their town. They will endlessly list off Akron places and activities they think you will enjoy and encourage you to check them out. There's really something beautiful in a community that seems to collectively wish to share what they pride, as if they don't want what's special to them to just be for them. But there was always a part of my heart still trapped in my beloved Southern California.

People were often perplexed over my attachment to the Blazer. Every time it needed work my buddy Chris would text me something to the effect of, "Who needs a new car? YOU need a new car! Buy a new fucking car!" I look at some of these service invoices from my years in Akron and I can hear Tim saying with reservation, "Are you sure you want to go ahead and do this job, E?" (Tim always calls me "E"). I gave him the green light every time. I spent $1,728.41 one time when Tim was with Fred Martin Chevrolet, Inc. In the top corner in his handwriting he had made the notation "rat." That was the job where during the diagnostic one of his mechanics found a dead, decaying rodent cradled in the innards of the Blazer's engine (Tim e-mailed me a picture of it that I still have). I can't find the invoice but I know at some point Tim had to replace the entire turn signal unit, not that people necessarily used that in Akron. Another $499.04 was spent when Tim was with Ron Marhofer Hyundai. Two years ago I threw down $798.53 on a steering/suspension job at Jeff's Motorcars, Inc., the high-end specialty shop where Tim finally settled as the assistant service manager. As my almost two-decade-old Blazer was being once again kept road-ready I strolled through the showroom filled with classic GTOs, Aston Martins, Mustangs, Corvettes, and Porsches. I felt like a teenager in a room full of girls that were far out of my league.

Now I'm finally going to confess. The irony is that once I arrived in Akron I really wasn't driving anywhere near the amount I had in Los Angeles, and yet the Blazer was falling apart. But I still felt at home when I was in it on the road. You see, in order to make the kind of life I wanted happen, I took the gamble a lot of academics do even though for the majority of them it doesn't pan out so well. For several years I ground it out as a "Freeway Flyer," taking any classes offered to me as a part-timer and going with no health insurance, or any benefits for that matter, other than the chance to build up my experience in the classroom. At one point I was in the Blazer as much as I was in front of students. One semester I was driving every week between Santa Monica College, Pierce College, West L.A. College, and Compton Community College. I would get books on CD or tape (yes, the Blazer had that function) and be in that truck hours on end. The Blazer became as much a part of my connection to the City of Angels as anything. So, if I never moved on to another car in Akron, if I kept the Blazer going, it meant I really wasn't staying in the Midwest. I could imagine selling my Akron house no problem, but I couldn't abandon the Blazer because, like me, it wasn't from here and maybe didn't belong. I even put a bumper sticker on it that proclaimed, "Stuck in Ohio!" just to reassure myself that this was all still temporary. There was no way of explaining this crazy line of thinking to anyone, so I just kept it to myself. I was convinced Midwesterners already thought I was nuts anyway, even the ones who had become close friends to the point of being surrogate family. I'm still trying to figure out this social ritual of making sure you're not the first person to reach for, say, the asparagus at a dinner party, or take the last tater tot in the basket when having beers with buddies.

Last summer the Blazer turned nineteen and I turned forty. As a birthday gift, my wife planned a great road trip that would take us from Akron to Louisville, down to Memphis, up to St. Louis, then through Iowa, spending Memorial Day weekend in Minneapolis with two of my brothers and their families, down to Madison to see a writing pal of mine, and eventually back to Akron. About 3,000-plus miles. Thea finally put her foot down and said she would not take the trip in the Blazer. She had visions of it permanently breaking down as we drove by cornfields in the middle of nowhere with the nearest service station being a hundred miles away. I told her I thought the Blazer could make it. In truth, I had my own doubts. It had recently developed an interesting sound coming from the dashboard whenever I was turning, like a small animal groaning then fading into a wheeze as the truck straightened out.

With reluctance and even a bit of defeat, I called up Tim and told him the time had come. I'm not sure he really believed me. Nevertheless, he put me in touch with his saleswoman friend, Ciarra, at Ron Marhofer Hyundai, whom he said was very honest and that I could trust to treat me well. Both proved true. I ended up buying a 2015 Hyundai Santa Fe Sport, even spent extra for the all-wheel drive now that I had experienced plenty of Northeast Ohio winters. I had Thea pick the new car's color. Ciarra said that Hyundai was a Korean company but that my new Santa Fe Sport was indeed American-made, that the factory was in Alabama. Still, I knew I would never again get the Midwestern street cred the Blazer had provided me since moving to Akron.

As for the Blazer itself, I considered keeping it for Home Depot runs or firewood hauls, but in the end, I decided it was time to let it go. The dealership trade-in expert took a first look at it and offered me an insulting $400. I felt I needed to defend the Blazer's honor. I had all those service invoices from Tim over the years in hand but the guy didn't want to see them. The six-CD changer was now obsolete and wouldn't impress him. So, I decided to pop the hood and make him at least look. His eyes actually did kind of bubble. He bent his head in and peered over the engine, started fingering things and said, "This is the cleanest engine I have ever seen in a nearly twenty-year-old Chevy. Kudos for regularly servicing your vehicle." I wanted to thank the academy for my performance being recognized, but I really had Tim to thank. In the end I got $1,800.00 for the Blazer. I didn't watch them drive it away. I knew it would be immediately sold at auction, probably for the parts alone. So, I drove my new Hyundai off the lot that day. And yes, I used my turn signal.

A funny thing happened during the two-week road trip Thea and I went on for my fortieth birthday. I started missing Akron. But more importantly, I started missing my Akron friends. I'm not a big postcard guy, but I started mailing postcards back home to those friends. I sent images of the places Thea and I were visiting: Elvis's Jungle Room at Graceland, Sun Records Studios, the supposed future birthplace of Captain Kirk, The St. Louis Arch, the farm where *Field of Dreams* was filmed, etc. All these spots we were driving to in my new car I had bought in Akron.

Somewhere between Madison and Akron, on the last stretch to home, Thea randomly asked me if I missed the Blazer. She was of course teasing me, but there was a little bit of seriousness there. In truth, I actually hadn't thought much about the Blazer the whole trip. But I had thought about Akron. I missed my adopted place. I missed my friends there even more.

And so, as that special trip concluded, we drove back into Akron in my brand new car that had not given us the slightest trouble over those 3,000-plus miles. At last I turned toward home. To the new house we'd bought, slightly off Market Street.

I pulled into the driveway and parked right over the oil drip stain in the concrete that had always been the Blazer's place. I cut the engine of my new car. We were back. I turned to Thea, saw how happy she was to be here again as well. This was now our place with our people. And it would be for a long time.

THE CAPITAL OF WEST VIRGINIA

By Patricia Fann

"What's the capital of West Virginia?" If you're a certain age and from Akron, you know that the punch line to this joke is not "Charleston," it's "Akron." That's because this question isn't about geography, it's about migration. It's about the tsunami of Appalachians who moved to Akron in the early twentieth century to escape a sinking economy and rising rivers. It's about those living in the backwoods and hills moving to a city with factories and paved streets and indoor plumbing. It's about people who were born and raised in Akron being alarmed by the seemingly endless influx of new people who had a different culture and way of talking. It's an "us" versus "them" statement veiled as humor.

Records show that Akron's population increased from 69,000 to 210,000, an increase of over 300 percent in ten years, from 1910 to 1920. Many of these migrants were people from Appalachia.

I have never thought this joke was funny, especially when I was a child growing up in Akron during the 1960s. It made me uncomfortable and I don't know why; maybe I didn't like the implied put-down. Maybe I didn't like the trick-question nature of it—that you had to be one of "us" to get it. Maybe I didn't like it because my father's family was from West Virginia and this joke, with its attached negative stereotype, didn't match up with what I knew about the Noffsingers. Now that I think about it, the joke made me ashamed to even tell people that I had family from West Virginia.

My grandpa, Frank Noffsinger, was from Red House, West Virginia. Red House is a small town tucked in the Appalachian mountains, on the banks of the Kanawha River, in Putnam County. It's on the western side of the state, just north of Charleston. In 2009, my husband, a few cousins, and I took my dad and his older brother and his wife back to Red House—the brothers hadn't been there since they were boys. The rest of us had never been there. Traveling the switchback roads on the mountains, I felt like I was in another country. We went for miles without seeing another soul. It is beautiful country, but you can't admire it too much while driving or you'll end up rolling down the side of the mountain. When we came upon a sign saying that we were getting close to Red House, we searched for anything that resembled a "downtown" or main part of town. Or an actual store. Or even a house. We saw mailboxes at the end of driveways, but the houses were hidden by the thick woods.

We drove around till we came to a modern, industrial-looking brick building identifying itself as the Red House Post Office and happened upon a middle-aged woman locking the building (it was after 3:00 in the afternoon by this time) who introduced herself as the postmistress. She was wearing typical, modern Postal Service attire, sensible shoes, and short-cropped hair—nothing like the high-necked Victorian dress, button-up shoes, and hair in a bun like you might imagine a postmistress would be sporting.

My 90-year-old, gregarious, and very charming dad got out of the car and became our unofficial spokesman. He told her we were Noffsingers from Ohio and that his father's family came from Red House. She directed us to the Noffsinger cemetery, across the street, right next to the Kanawha River. Amazing. In Akron there are very few people with our last name. In this tiny town, there's a whole cemetery of us. When we asked her about Noffsingers still living in

Red House, she told us there was one who ran the "hillbilly mart" up the road. But we spent a lot of time at the cemetery, so by the time we made it to the market (which, contrary to my expectations, was a nice, modern, generic-looking convenience store), we were told our relative had gone home for the day.

My Grandma Noffsinger was from Jarvisville, West Virginia, a small town in Harrison Country, northeast of Red House, high in the Appalachian Mountains. My dad told me that Grandma and Grandpa were introduced through the United Brethren Church. Grandma's father was a pastor in the UB church and Grandpa Noffsinger was a devout churchgoer. Because of the distance between their two towns (about 140 miles nowadays using highways and interstates that didn't exist then) it must have been an arduous and rarely made journey in the nineteenth century when they married. They got to know each other through letters. When it became clear that they were compatible, they married, and eventually settled in the bustling village of Middleport, Ohio (just across the Ohio River from West Virginia, near where the Kanawha empties into the Ohio), where they opened a general store. I have a picture from 1911 showing Grandma and Grandpa standing in the doorway of their store. They lived in the upstairs of the two-story, clapboard structure with their three young children, my aunts Wilma, Myrtis, and Eloise. By March of 1913, Grandma was pregnant with her fourth child, my Aunt Kathryn.

Easter Sunday, March 23, 1913, a "superstorm" began to cut across the United States producing tornadoes and floods unlike anything else seen before or since; it's estimated that more than one thousand people died from the storms and floods in the fourteen states affected. Although the Johnstown Flood of 1889 had caused more deaths (2,209 people according to Encyclopedia Britannica), in terms of sheer destruction and broadest effect, the 1913 storm was historic. By some accounts, the Ohio River rose a foot an hour, breaking through levees, driving people to higher ground. Many died trying to find higher ground. About 50 miles upriver of Middleport, in Marietta, the National Weather Service records show that the Ohio River crested to 58.30 feet on March 29, 1913, a record that stands to this day. Official flood level of the Ohio River in Marietta is 35 feet.

Fortunately, my grandparents and their three small children were able to escape to their second floor where they were rescued by boat from a bedroom window. Even though all escaped alive, this experience understandably left Grandma with a fear of water and flooding. She vowed to never again live someplace that could flood. With their store destroyed, hearing stories of plentiful jobs up north, and with five mouths to feed and another baby on the way, Grandpa followed the well-worn route from Appalachia to the Akron area. Once he found a job and place to live (initially in Cuyahoga Falls), he sent for Grandma and their four little girls. Of course, Akron and the Ohio Canal suffered from the devastating effects of the 1913 flood as well, but to someone who has seen the Ohio River swallow up her home and business, I imagine that Grandma liked the sound of Summit County, and Akron, which comes from the Greek word for "high point" or "elevation." Perhaps coincidentally, they moved to North Hill, which although not the highest point in Summit County, might have given Grandma an additional sense of elevation and safety. North Hill had the advantage of being a quick streetcar ride from Grandpa's job as a rubber worker at B. F. Goodrich, and, perhaps most importantly, the family was within walking distance of their United Brethren Church on East Tallmadge Avenue (now the International Institute). My dad and his siblings loved growing up in North Hill.

To this day, over a hundred years later, North Hill is still a welcoming neighborhood for those fleeing poverty and danger in their homelands, and looking for a better life for their families. According to statistics from the City of Akron, 6.6% of North Hill residents are foreign born compared to 1.1% for Akron overall, and 4.2% of North Hill residents report that they speak English not well or not at all compared to 1.5% for Akron overall.

Although my grandparents were from West Virginia, they did not match the stereotype of uneducated "hillbillies" who lived in shacks in the hills, had a casual approach to bathing and dental hygiene, and distilled their own, ahem, alcoholic refreshment. Not that there's anything wrong with that. Grandma was the daughter of a

minister. Grandpa was a school teacher before taking up store keeping, and was strictly anti-alcohol. Their wedding picture shows a very serious-looking, plain but well-dressed young couple. I didn't know my grandparents well, but my dad told me that Grandpa's nickname at the rubber factory was "Doc" because he was such a sober, well-read sort of person. Grandma didn't go anywhere without a hat, gloves, and jewelry. During the Depression in the early twentieth century, "hoboes" were welcomed into Grandma and Grandpa's kitchen on Dayton Street. Grandma fed them while Grandpa read the Bible aloud. My dad and all his siblings graduated from high school. My Aunt Wilma graduated from Akron City Hospital's registered nurse program. My other aunts became secretaries for the family doctor and helped support the family during the Depression. My aunts Myrtis and Eloise were very talented musically and played piano and sang at church and on one of the many religious radio shows on the air in Akron during the 1930s. My uncle Frank became an engineer for Ohio Bell. My dad attended the University of Chicago but didn't earn his degree due to a family emergency that brought him home his senior year. He worked at Polsky's department store in downtown Akron, as a carpet salesman.

Though not wealthy, the family was respectable and very literate. Dad and his brother served with honor in World War II.

Of course, my grandparents' decision to move to Akron determined my existence, since my parents met here. But, having West Virginian roots has come in handy a few times, I must admit. There was the time in the 1970s I was working as a secretary at a nursing home in Fairlawn and one of my duties was to have the patients sign documents each month. The woman training me said that there was one woman, Lucy Hinkle, who always refused to sign and that the previous secretary just signed for her, rather than confront her. The nurses told me Lucy was not only stubborn and obstinate, but yelled and threw things at people. They said she was cantankerous but there was nothing wrong with her mind. Signing her name for her as if she had dementia didn't seem right to me so, armed with the moral compass of my ancestors, and all the courage my 20-year-old self could muster, I found her room on the second floor and opened the door. There sat an alert woman with long white hair, an angular face, and wiry build. She was in a wheelchair, but was still imposing and intimidating. I told her what I wanted and why. She demanded to know my name and my politics, accusing me (and everyone there) of being a Communist. When I assured her I was not a Communist and told her my full name, she paused for a moment and said she knew some Noffsingers and wanted to know where "my people" were from. When I told her, it turned out she was from Jarvisville, knew my grandma, and was at my grandparents wedding. She told me my great-grandfather had red hair and my grandma had a fiery temper, two things later confirmed by family stories and pictures. She then told me her life's story and she and I became friends. She signed those documents that month and every month thereafter, and she called me "her girl." I learned that having family from West Virginia could help you build connections with people in Akron.

My West Virginian ancestry may have unconsciously played a role in my own marriage. My mother-in-law's family is from Bridgeport, Ohio, and Martins Ferry, Ohio (both just across the Ohio River from Wheeling, West Virginia). When my husband and I were dating, this was not something I remember discussing, but I can't help but wonder if our common Appalachian roots gave us some shared values that has helped build our 35-year-plus marriage.

Reading Karl Grismer's book *Akron and Summit County*, I was struck by the absence of West Virginians in his "Biographies" section of influential Akronites up through 1952, when the book was written. Surely, such a large group must have produced some ambitious people who shaped our city? Judging by his list, the city was run mostly by white men whose roots were in Connecticut and New York. He does mention the stereotype of the West Virginian "Snake Eater" (apparently it was thought that snakes comprised a large part of the diet of West Virginians) who worked at the rubber shops, but Mr. Grismer doesn't spend much time on this group of people. Surprising. However, I found Susan Allyn Johnson's PhD dissertation, entitled "Industrial Voyagers: A Case Study of Appalachian Migration to Akron, Ohio 1900-1940," online, and it was less dismissive of West Virginians. Dr. Johnson talks about the fact that the influence of West Virginians on Akron culture has not been written about very much. She puts forth the theory that many local historians thought that most migrants made their money in the rubber shops then returned to their home towns. She acknowledges that this was not the case and gives some excellent examples of ways that Appalachians influenced our music, our neighborhoods, our churches, and our customs.

There were many, like my family, who moved from Appalachia to Akron and made Akron a better place; these were people who brought their intelligence, resourcefulness, music, folk art, work ethic, and pragmatism with them as they crossed mountains and rivers. To be sure, some of them matched the stereotype and I'm certain their descendants are rightly proud of their colorful and uniquely American ancestors. So as I learn more about the contributions of these migrants, I see this joke in a different way today. I choose to think of it as recognition of the impact that those people—*my* people—had on a city I love so much. I like to think it is shorthand for how the people from West Virginia built the neighborhoods, filled the schools and churches, and produced the goods that made Akron so vibrant. Their influence lives on, and I'm proud to be the granddaughter of West Virginians.

HAPPY, HAPPY JESUS HELLO

By Matthew Meduri

Akron will never be known as the Rapture City. There've never been groups of people vanishing into the sky. No four horsemen galloping through Quaker Square. No second coming of Christ, unless you're a Cavs fan. However, when I was eleven years old, I witnessed the most dramatic and visceral rendering of this apocalyptic event in none other than Ernest Angley's Grace Cathedral, a mere footnote in this area's history.

Growing up as the son of a "recovering" Catholic, born-again Christian pastor and a Methodist mother, I was no stranger to the stories and teachings of the Bible. While most folks were either part of the Christmas-Easter rush or the faithful Sunday crowd, to some capacity my life was church. We were by no means fire-and-brimstone fundamentalists like those who protest abortion clinics or stand on the corner of an intersection telling people to abandon their wicked ways (well, that may have happened once or twice). We were just your average white, midwestern Protestants, so God with a capital G was part of our everyday lives. As kids, my little brother and I felt like we were always at church for something: the service, a hymn sing, a potluck, cleaning. My parents held weekly Bible study or prayer group at our house, and we prayed at every meal and read from the Bible at bedtime. When other children were reading Mother Goose, Hans Christian Andersen, and Roald Dahl, we read about David and Goliath, Jonah and the whale, and Daniel and the lions' den. Sure there was time for video games, sports, sleepovers, and pop culture-saturated TV, as long as you snuck in a psalm or beatitude from time to time. So needless to say, when family friends from church asked us to go to a play about the rapture, we had a fairly good idea of what we had accepted or at least we thought we did.

Tim and Debbie weren't just any fellow parishioners. They were the fun, easy-going people who didn't pretend to be saints. They would tell raunchy jokes, occasionally swear, talk about the not-so-Christian days of their youth without shame, and order pizza when I'd come over to hang out with their son who was a year older. He rode BMX, had one of those awful undercut, pre man-bun ponytails, and was a pathological liar (he once said he had dodged a drive-by shooting at his home in Niles by jumping behind a line of trashcans)—basically an insufferable shit who, at the time, I thought was cool. They always seemed to be going to Christian rock concerts, funny movies, slightly more charismatic church services, the kind where people are waving flags, falling on the floor, and speaking nonsense. Perhaps it was an unusual form of entertainment for them or maybe an opportunity to visit the fringe of Christian culture without having to drink the Kool-Aid, per se. If they were going somewhere or doing something, it was safe to say that it was going to be a good time. None of us questioned their offer of free tickets to a play, because we would probably get a decent meal and enjoy ourselves.

At this point in my life at age eleven, Ernest Angley was a national and even internationally known televangelist, akin to the likes of Oral Roberts, Jim Bakker, Pat Robertson, Jerry Falwell, or Jimmy Swaggart. I'd heard his name several times from the older folks at church, some of whom had even been to one of the services at the illustrious Grace Cathedral. But I knew this white-suit-wearing Southerner with a bad toupee mainly from his post-primetime program *The Ninety and Nine Club*. He always greeted the viewer with, "And a happy, happy Jesus hello to all you out there tonight," in a drawl that made Jesus sound like *Jeezuz*. I thought his manner of speech was part of the televangelist persona, and of course it was, but later I found out that like many Akronites, Ernie was a transplant, an out-of-towner. He and his wife came from North Carolina as traveling faith healers, which explains his end-of-show, post-donation mantra. "Heal. Heal. Heeeal."

Ernie's Akron empire, or compound, encompassed Grace Cathedral and a tall concrete towere erected by his predecessor, Rex Humbard. The massive cylinder was supposed to house a rotating restaurant at the top, but due to some legal issues, construction was abandoned and Humbard left for Florida (a very Ohioan move) to continue his more lucrative ministry. Dubbed "Rex's Erection," this symbol will forever linger in this region's psyche. Yet the towering phallus never obstructed Ernie's vision. He has done his best to make the place his own. He added a buffet that was never really able to compete with Ponderosa or Golden Corral, but does have a wax museum in its basement, depicting the life of Jesus. The place is no Madame Tussauds, but it does rival the typical rigged stuffed animal claw machine for buffet restaurant entertainment. Angley's weekly television show, *The Ernest Angley Hour*, replaced Humbard's *Cathedral of Tomorrow*. The show typically depicted Angley and his entourage at a revival in Africa, a place he travelled to in his own private jet. There he claimed to cure lines of people of AIDS by putting his hands on them and shouting, "Be healed in the name of Jeezuz." People would shake and dance and flop on the ground, a sign that they were indeed healed. I was never hugely adept in the sciences, but even as an 11-year-old, I thought Ernie's necromancer powers were dubious at best. The only person I had heard of at the time who could cure AIDS, or rather HIV, was Magic Johnson. But to top off the Humbard/Angley legacy of strange, rumor has it that when Ernie's wife died, he had a telephone placed in her coffin, which was then buried under a statue at the location of his other church not far from Akron. The implication of this act seems clear but what exactly did it signify regarding Ernie?

The evening of the show came and we were ready. Our family (minus my father, who was busy) hopped in our red '95 Ford Windstar and met Tim and Debbie and their son at the front door of Grace Cathedral. Inside, the sanctuary was much larger than I had expected. Rows of blue chairs were arranged before a large stage with red-carpeted stairs and white pillars, cloaked by large red curtains, hiding the actors and props. On the ceiling was an enormous red and white lighted cross, a fixture I could not take my eyes off of as we made our way to our seats. The lighting made the place feel expansive. I felt a little dizzy.

Eventually the lights dimmed, and the stage spots went up on a man, yet the red cross remained illuminated. The man in the spotlight introduced the play, but he was not Ernie. No, he was likely one of the associate pastors or some staff member of the church. My confusion quickly turned to disappointment. "Where's Ernest Angley?" I asked my mother. She shrugged her shoulders, saying,

"Maybe he's on a mission trip." The answer satisfied my suspicion, but I wondered why a play so popular (as I looked around the place was nearly full) would not be introduced by the author himself. It's not that I really liked the guy or anything, but after years of seeing the man on television, I felt like he would have been at his own play based on his own novel at his own church. So much for pride of authorship. The man walked off stage and the red cross dimmed until it was just a silhouette in the ceiling, a shadow cross.

The curtain was pulled away.

Now, a quick note on Angley's *Raptured*. Written as a novel in 1950, it depicted what the world would look like after Jesus takes the faithful up to heaven. This one event comes from Revelation, one of the most cryptic and hotly debated books in the Bible. Supposedly written by the apostle John on the island of Patmos, it depicted a vision of the end of the world given by Jesus. The book is full of confusing references and bizarre imagery: beasts, scrolls, seals (not the aquatic animal), horsemen, witnesses, bowls, dragons, Jesus in a red robe stained with the blood of martyrs, an antichrist, a whore of Babylon, a New Heaven and Earth. Unknowingly, as preparation for this play, I had watched a year or so prior a movie called *A Thief in the Night*, the *Easy Rider* to what would later become a film genre, depicting these very same events. I was ready for this.

The play began with a single man waking up to find the person close to him no longer there. In a subtle frenzy he searched but to no avail. Then he turned on the television to discover a significant portion of the world's population was gone. I knew this opening; it was basically the opening to the movie I had watched a year earlier. But despite the similarities, I wasn't bored. I was actually kind of wondering what would happen next. It was something familiar and suspenseful and even kind of exciting. Ernie was an entertainer who knew how to keep you on the edge of your seat. He got the ball rolling, so to speak, and an hour and a half of chaos ensued.

This was not a play of redemption. This was what happened when you were not ready for the Second Coming of Christ. And guess what? It was only doom and destruction and pain, even for the people who realized the error of their ways and converted. So much for everlasting love.

Some actors were arrested, others branded with the mark of the beast (666). The main character did his best to avoid all of this, but even though he had asked for forgiveness and became a Christian, realized eventually he would to have to pay for his fatal flaw, the mistake of not believing beforehand, of not being ready. The people who resisted being branded with the mark were beaten rather violently and convincingly. Those who took the mark appeared exponentially more sinister.

Every so often I glanced at our friends, who seemed entertained, even captivated. But my little brother was wide-eyed, and my mother was cringing at the more gruesome parts. I remember wondering what my father would have thought at this moment. Would he have been as shocked as the three of us, possibly suggesting we leave? Or would he have seen this as a spiritual moment, a personal revelation from God, an act of edification? It was difficult to know, but I do know he would have been right here telling us we had nothing to be afraid of. We wouldn't have to experience any of these events. Those things won't happen to believers. Unfortunately, he wasn't there that night, and in a way, I was experiencing these events. I was part of the show.

Then in Ernie's play, I saw a person beheaded. He walked up to a sleek metal guillotine and slid his head into place. Unfortunately, or perhaps fortunately, the victim's head was obscured by the design of the guillotine. The large blade dropped and although I couldn't see the actual beheading, I heard the sound, a familiar sound used in many horror movies, the sound of a head being lopped off, a blade through a nice trunk of flesh and cartilage. Without warning, a head that looked exactly like that person, bloody stump and all, rolled down a ramp, Mayan style. I didn't expect that kind of special effects or gore in a Christian play at a televangelist's church in Ohio. The crowd gasped. My brother and mother gaped. The beheadings continued one after another until the main character lost his as well. I didn't see that coming. Sure, he was going to die, but maybe it would have been implied? Whatever happened to dimming the lights and closing the curtain? Angley certainly had not taken the Hitchcock approach to horror. Why had he wanted us to see the head?

Tim looked to my mother and told her to turn around. From the back of the church, walking through the door of the sanctuary was a man draped in a long black cloak. The spotlight was on him, and as he approached I could see the numbers "666" stamped on his forehead. The Antichrist. The contacts in his eyes resembled those of Marilyn Manson. He stared down members of the audience and asked people if they would either take his mark or join the fate of those on stage. I glanced at my mother, and she looked terrified. My brother was petrified. I felt very uneasy. If only my father were in the aisle seat as a buffer between that man and our family. He might have suggested leaving. No excuses, no shame. He would never have put on a play like this in his church, in our church. Instead of scaring people into what the future might look like, he would have told us how we could live a better life, a happier life. But I was not with my father. I was in this crowded stadium of a church, and my only choice was to endure another 20 minutes of horror until the curtain closed.

Finally, the Antichrist left, and the play resumed. There was one final scene, in which I couldn't really tell what was happening because at this point the lighting and special effects and sound were so great that I had slouched in my seat, placed my hand to my brow like a person does when shading his eyes from the sun. I could only observe peripherally. The downfall of this technique was that I could still hear the noises and the screaming, and my curiosity was real. So I looked. There stood something straight out of Greek mythology or, more appropriately, the book of Revelation—an animatronic beast with the body of a lion, the wings of an eagle, the face of a man with jagged teeth, and the tail of a scorpion. This beast was stinging people left and right. People were screaming. There was blood. The lights flashed and smoke was everywhere. Slowly the stage lights faded, along with the sound, and eventually the curtains closed.

Applause.

I don't remember really talking about what had happened in there on the ride home or why we stayed the entire time, clearly terrified by the spectacle. Even when I brought it up years later, as

I began to sort of sift through past events due to a sudden interest in Rapture Culture, my mother and brother both said they didn't remember much about the play, like they put it out of their minds. I recall having this unsettling fear that I wasn't ready for the Rapture, and if it did happen I would likely be left behind. Did I have enough faith? Then again, would I have been strong enough to say no to the mark of the beast?

At night, lying in bed, I was fearful that I wouldn't hear the trumpet call, but rather the clopping of the hooves of the Four Horsemen and perhaps have to go into hiding. The aftermath of Angley's play was like watching a horror movie, and then thinking Freddy Krueger was around every corner. The only real difference was that people don't believe in Freddy Krueger.

It's difficult to say whether or not my father approved of our outing. He didn't have the opportunity to see the show, or our expressions that night. Despite the boundaries televangelists tend to push while making spectacles of themselves (if they didn't, no one would watch), I know my father might not approve of their delivery of the message. Nevertheless, he still believes (like many) in its content, because it is his truth. And what is true is good, right? This is likely why he later had us watch the very dull *Left Behind* movies starring the even less impressive Kirk Cameron when they came out, and why he continues to preach about the events in Revelation, albeit with less fervor than someone like Ernie. Regardless of the enormous number of Rapture hoaxes perpetrated by well-known religious charlatans, a significant number of people believe the events portrayed in that play will happen, and in their lifetime. So when I asked my father what he thought when we told him about the show, and our relative trauma, he said, ironically, "I would have never have let you go to something like that if I'd have known." His look and tone made it clear that maybe it wasn't such a good idea. But then again, you don't have anything to be afraid of if you believe.

BF

By Liesl Schwabe

In the cramped darkroom on the fourth floor of my high school, I waited next to a junior named Adam while our pictures floated in the developer, already regretting that we would not be having furtive sex on the counter between the enlargers. As the charge of adolescent possibility reverberated in the thin red light, we stood with our tongs in the chemicals. But I was resigned to my own predictable habits. It was never going to happen. The entirety of my teenage life seemed to consist of sensing potential and then chickening out. I was cautious, in the National Honor Society, and captain of the swim team. Instead, we watched the images blooming in our trays.

"Where is that?" Adam asked, looking at my picture of a row of broken factory windows.

"The B.F. Goodrich building," I said. And for the moment, the satisfaction of my answer overtook the suspended lament I always felt for being so good. For being the kind of girl who did not make passes at anyone ever, but especially not while pictures of his cheerleader girlfriend emerged with a benevolent smile below. Even though I was almost positive he would have been game.

In the spring of 1993, I was 17 years old and in my final months at Cuyahoga Falls High School. Locally known as "Caucasian Falls," the Akron suburb where I lived was the archetype of American mediocrity: all aluminum siding and sidewalks no one walked on, well-tended but uninviting. A lower socioeconomic strata existed, but for the most part, folks were solidly middle-middle-class, suspicious of anyone with significantly more or less. My high school wasn't bad, but it wasn't good either. There was a general expectation that kids do well enough to get into Akron U. or Kent State, but there was just as much of an expectation for them not to go looking any farther.

I knew whose family was Catholic and whose family was Protestant; of those, I knew who was Methodist, Lutheran, or fundamentalist. Like everything else, though, church was to be respected but not taken too seriously. No one wanted anyone going and getting all devout or weird. Especially when everyone had seen each other at the drive-thru buying beers on Saturday night. *Enlightenment* of any sort was frowned upon, not unlike foreign cuisine and ambition.

The margin for what was acceptable seemed narrower than a carefully mowed devil's strip, and I felt neither capable of stepping outside of it nor of remaining where I was supposed to. I desperately wanted to become a more interesting version of myself, but I had no idea how. My parents had graduated from the same school I was then attending, and I lifeguarded at the same pool where they had also worked. The same football games, swim meets, and black and gold varsity letters that defined my life had once defined theirs, with nothing, it seemed, to disrupt the unsurprising continuity of our suburban eternity. The Dairy Queen and the Sparkle Market and the Krispy Kreme were as immutable to the landscape as the Cuyahoga River itself. Because there was nowhere else, it appeared, to go.

The one exception, I discovered my senior year, was down the road, over the high level bridge, and through the deserted streets of downtown Akron, to what those of us who went there referred to as "BF."

In 1871, Benjamin Franklin Goodrich opened the rubber factory that bore his name. By the years following World War II, when my parents were growing up in what would become fleeting Midwestern prosperity, Akron had become the rubber capital of the world, and the vast majority of the tires produced then came out of the three-million-square-foot factory that was the B.F. Goodrich Company plant. For decades, tire production in Akron was so abundant that the acrid smell of burning rubber hung in the air. Until, like most American manufacturing along what had been the Erie Canal, the whole industry evaporated or moved away, taking with it the jobs and the unions that had made the area thrive for a century. In 1986, B.F. Goodrich closed its Akron doors.

Empty and abandoned, the enormous brick building sat exposed to the elements for years. From the outside, it looked not unlike the apocalyptic remnants of some nuclear holocaust. Inside, each floor was bigger than a football field, a wide expanse of cement and rubble, with two-toned columns still holding up the ceiling. Most, but not all of the windows were broken. Some exterior walls had entire sections missing, meaning it was possible to stand at the edge of the fifth floor with nothing to hold you in. But somewhere around the third or fourth story, one level was left oddly intact. With walls, windows, and an endless, uncluttered cement floor—ideal for plywood ramps and small half-pipes—BF became a clandestine clubhouse for skaters. Squeezing through the bent chain link fence and climbing up the open concrete staircase for the first time, I felt not only the thrill of the forbidden, but something deeper and truer to what I craved: reinvention.

Much like the idea of losing my virginity, the idea of trespassing with skaters had been a source of anticipation and desperate wonder for years. When I was eleven, the drained pool of a neglected hotel near my house was taken over by boys with asymmetrical hair and ruggedly elegant Vision Streetwear high-tops. I rode my bike down an alley from which I could watch them without their seeing me in return. With their boards teetering on the edge of the cement abyss, those boys were ablaze with their youth, preoccupied with nothing, fast and certain. I both wanted them and wanted to be them. They were defiant and beautiful and nonchalant. And I was what I had always been, curious and observant and safely out of sight.

Six years later, the B.F. Goodrich version of that scene wasn't quite as sexy. There were puddles on the floor and no lights. The battery-operated boom box playing Dinosaur Jr. was never quite loud enough to provide the soundtrack that seemed it ought to have been playing. Though someone was always shaking a can of Krylon, none of the graffiti was very good, just the messy, overlapping evidence of teenage frustration. But initially brought by my skater boyfriend and realizing I wanted something to do other than watch him and a dozen other guys in flannel shirts try to land kick-flips, BF was also where I started to take pictures. Where I began to experiment with composition, with what parts of the story could be omitted or left out of focus.

Most of the pictures I took there turned out pretty badly, grey and muted in the damp March light. And eyeing all the other boys more closely than the one whose coat I was holding, I knew I was already bored with my own boyfriend, that I liked driving to BF with him more than I liked driving back to his house after. But none of that mattered as much as being there. Because this time, I hadn't stayed outside the fence, looking in, and in doing so, I was laying claim to a different kind of inheritance.

Downtown Akron had always been haunted by an air of loss, by something we couldn't name and maybe couldn't even imagine. A time when the elusive history our parents told us about—the Christmas windows at Polsky's and the Wurlitzer pipe organ coming out of the stage during intermission at the grand Civic Theatre—wasn't just a vague specimens of someone else's nostalgia. Because as far as our generation could see, the buildings were falling apart and the buses on Main Street had no people in them. We didn't really believe it had ever been otherwise.

But unlike Cuyahoga Falls, which seemed committed to preserving its own static predictability along with the verdure of its lawns, Akron was striking, even scary, for the texture of extremes it provided, most notably that of erratic change. Even if we couldn't envision a downtown filled with happy, well-dressed families and men earning livable salaries, we were compelled by the architecture of their ghosts. And so the old factory offered this strange threshold not only into the lusty world of teenage boys with flat stomachs and scraped elbows, but into the very notion that change was possible. That what had been one thing could become something else.

We were teenagers. We didn't care or understand what a closed factory meant. We couldn't think in consequences, and we were not yet burdened by the need for a job or a faith in our country. Which was why BF was broken but magic, a place where possibility and chance did not have to be summoned, but simply were. Metamorphosis in process, not unlike being seventeen. Not unlike watching a photograph develop. Not unlike a kick-flip.

FORECLOSURES AND VAMPIRE DEVILS:

A GUIDE TO BUYING A HOME IN AKRON

By Chris Drabick

The official word is that, upon entering the unlocked home on Sand Run Road, Akron police found fifty-year-old Henry "Hi" Heepe in bed with parts of his mother's corpse during the late evening hours of November 8, 1994. Unofficially, it's pretty easy to read between the lines and see that "in bed" is the polite way to say that Hi may have been engaged in the sort of carnal pursuits frowned upon even with one's living parent.

It'd be bad enough if that were the entirety of the story, but another officer found an eyeball staring back at him from the toilet, a third discovered what seemed to be various body parts boiling in a pot on the stove. There was blood on Hi's mouth. It was assumed he'd ingested some of his mom.

Upon interrogation, Hi claimed he'd "cut out both of her hearts," the unfortunate seventy-seven-year-old Barbara Heepe being pegged by her obviously disturbed son as a "vampire devil." "She took a lot of killing," Hi told the authorities, which explains why a young neighbor boy who was raking leaves heard Barbara screaming for help many hours before they'd found the pair. She'd been beaten, strangled, and stabbed over fifty times.

As one might expect, it took many, many months before they found a buyer for the house on Sand Run Road.

I'd fought off adulthood for longer than most, but as I neared my forties I'd happily settled down with my wife Alison. Nick Hornby wrote in *High Fidelity* that "it's not what you're like, it's what you like," and it's safe to say that I might have put more weight into those words than is either healthy or advisable. But Alison had also read her share of Nick Hornby.

With that in mind, my new wife and I were in agreement about lots of things, especially when it came to aesthetics. That included what we were looking for as we shopped for our first home; we wanted something older and with character, hardwood floors, crown molding, lots of space. The sort of place to start a family. We'd been renting in the Wallhaven neighborhood of West Akron, and we liked its mix of retirees and young families and walkable feel, and wanted to stay near there. I'd been quite taken with Castle Boulevard, a tree-lined stretch of uniformly well-kept old Colonials and Tudors near our rental, but the single house for sale on the street was acceptable only to me. To be fair, I probably liked it mostly due to the fact that I really wanted to live on Castle Boulevard.

So with the help of our experienced real estate agent Betty, we expanded our search to cover wider swaths of West Akron and even peeked across the city border into Fairlawn (but just barely). In 2011, there was no shortage of priced-to-sell housing stock in the area; we were perfectly situated for a bargain.

We saw the most expensive house for sale amongst the more modest and downright rough homes on Marvin Avenue, just south of Market Street, as well as the least expensive house on upscale Sunnyside—a ranch monstrosity that would've looked shitty on Marvin. We looked at ranches and split-levels, untouched mid-centuries in need of major updates and foreclosures in need of demolition. Alison liked the quirky place in Highland Square, I liked the one on Winston Avenue that we couldn't afford (I thought we could get the price down; it sold for asking). We looked at dozens of houses. I think Betty was getting tired of us as the search took us to the blue Colonial on Sand Run.

By the time we saw it, it had changed hands a couple more times after the murder, including after the housing crash, when it had been foreclosed upon and, according to the then-current owner/occupant, completely stripped and decently trashed by the unlucky, angry soul who'd overspent at the height of the market.

The owner bought it on the cheap from Deutsche Bank and then spent thousands updating the kitchen, bathrooms, and floors. He put in a full bathroom on the first floor. There was a hot tub, a nice two-car garage, plenty of space. Sand Run Road is nicely located, close to shopping and the Metro Parks. Although I disliked the lack of sidewalks in that area of town, I was willing to overlook it for so much underpriced, move-in-ready house. We were tired of looking. No house was going to be perfect.

In the days and weeks following the murder on Sand Run, the national press predictably picked up the story, and various accounts of the gruesome scene found their way from sea to shining sea, even stopping for a few updates in my college newspaper. I don't remember reading about it at the time, which is odd considering my mild obsession with Jeffrey Dahmer's trail of terror a few years before (maybe Henry didn't leave enough victims for me to notice).

Had I paid attention, I'd have read that Henry Heepe was declared by Common Pleas judge Jane Bond not guilty by reason of insanity in April of 1995. Judge Bond, obviously shaken by the details of the case, commented that the murder on Sand Run was an incident in which "the veil of sanity drops and we are all given a glimpse into the abyss." Hi was sent to the Moritz Forensic Center in Columbus, where he'd stay either until death, or a state declaration that he was sane. This was followed by news that he'd sued his mother's estate for a chunk of her life insurance policy. Hi's successful insanity plea, and subsequent technical innocence in the death of his mother, was the only thing allowing said suit to move forward. Henry was a smoker, and complained that he had no money for cigarettes. There was an undisclosed settlement, but the promise of staying flush with Marlboros at Moritz was not enough to keep Hi alive. He hung himself on November 6, 1995, just two days before the anniversary of his mother's death. There is no official word, but it's hard to imagine the two events are unrelated.

As I recall, Betty never directly told us about the house's history. She whispered something or other about certain buyers being hesitant about the place, and whatever she said was enough to get one or both of us poking around the internet to discover the real reason behind the home's bargain price. Or so we believed.

It wasn't enough to scare us. In fact, Alison and I embraced the house's history. No other couples we knew had this sort of conversation starter about their home. Neither of us believed in ghosts. Besides, the home had been trashed and stripped and remodeled, so it's not as though the toilet was the same toilet that held Barbara

Heepe's eyeball, nor was it the same stove where Hi had warmed up a portion of his mom's innards. We regaled ourselves with the endless possibilities for the greatest Halloween parties anyone would know, where only I would don the traditional costume of vampire devil. We'd talked ourselves into The Murder House.

Upon inspection, there proved to be ghosts of a different sort in the form of a bad foundation that would cost tens of thousands to repair. We walked away from the purchase. Alison was more upset than I was at the time, but whatever loss either of us felt turned to joy less than forty-eight hours later as a wonderful home on Castle Boulevard went on the market. We saw it and bought it that same day.

By now, we've filled our house on Castle Boulevard with two boys, and I've done more—but not all—of my growing up. My pre-fatherhood fantasies of amazing Halloween parties have been replaced by relief that I'll never have to explain to Augie and Elliott who Henry Heepe was.

For Halloween 2015, I did not dress as a vampire devil. Instead, I spent trick or treat night the same way I have for the last five years; I passed out candy to the Olafs and Elsas, the Minions and Chewbaccas. It's more sedate than I might have imagined; there's no tomato juice-based punch, human organ soup, or other Heepe party accouterments we might have concocted.

I couldn't be happier. We didn't buy the Heepe house, but if I believed in ghosts, I might think Hi and his mom were looking out for us.

SNAPSHOTS FROM A ROCK 'N' ROLL MARRIAGE

By Denise Grollmus
Previously published in Salon.

1. Tin Huey T-Shirt

The day Patrick asked me for a divorce, I was wearing our Tin Huey T-shirt.

It is charcoal gray and the softest cotton, thanks to decades of wear. The neck is perfectly stretched out. Just above my collar bone, there is a tear along the stitching, giving the illusion that the rest of the shirt might spontaneously unravel and fall from my body, leaving me with nothing but a ribbed cotton necklace. There are holes everywhere: under the armpits, around my torso, on my back. My favorite hole is the one along the stitching of the left sleeve, forcing it to drape down over my left bicep and expose my shoulder, as though it were some elegantly crafted evening dress. Still faintly legible across the chest is "TIN HUEY" in stenciled, white acrylic letters, cracked throughout like an antique vase. No matter how much you wash it, it smells like people, rather than detergent. I don't wash it often, because I don't want it to disintegrate.

The shirt first came into Patrick's possession in 2003, when his band, the Black Keys, started garnering national attention, including a spot as the musical guest on *Late Night With Conan O'Brien*. Tin Huey's guitarist gave it to Patrick hoping he would wear it on the show. It would be an honor, Patrick said. Patrick was obsessed with any rock band that ever came out of Akron, Ohio—from big names like Devo and Chrissie Hynde to little-known acts like Chi-Pig, the Bizarros, and, of course, Tin Huey. His uncle Ralph had played saxophone in the band. Patrick remembers his grandparents always playing their only major label release, *Contents Dislodged During Shipment*, on the hi-fi. But it wasn't simply the band's sound that enchanted Patrick. It was the possibility of creating something special in a seemingly unspecial town like Akron—a place where people are not known for making art but for manufacturing tires. He cherished records like the Waitresses' *Wasn't Tomorrow Wonderful?* because they were definitive proof that maybe he could do the same.

The night Patrick first appeared on national television, I remember thinking, "I will never forget this moment." Sadly, more than seven years later, I have. In order to jog my memory, I search the

Internet for a video of the performance. After several hours of sifting through the myriad of music videos, interviews and national TV appearances the Black Keys have made since, I begin to doubt that the moment ever happened at all—that I had made it up entirely. But then, I find it—a three-minute, thirty-four-second snippet of the Black Keys performing on *Conan O'Brien*, August 8, 2003.

The video clip begins just as Conan is saying "... guests from Akron, Ohio." The audience's cheers quickly fade into the signature riff of "Thickfreakness"—a cascade of reverb echoing from the guitar of Pat's bandmate, Dan Auerbach. I know that riff well—I've heard it, literally, hundreds of times. I know when Dan has hit the wrong note, slyly sliding the fuzz into the right one. I also know when Patrick hits in too soon or too late on his drum kit. On *Conan*, I notice that he hits in too early and is playing the song too fast, probably because he is nervous. Dan is forced to catch up. The audience probably has no idea—but I do. Even seven years later.

When the camera finally pans away from Dan singing, I see that Patrick is, in fact, wearing the Tin Huey shirt and I'm ecstatic by this vindication. My memory is no fake. But my victory is too quickly displaced by a sudden surge of tears that surprise me as they stream down my cheeks. He looks so young. Our T-shirt is not yet full of holes. It fits him perfectly—hugging his tall, fit frame. I can tell that I gave him the haircut he is sporting. I can remember how I used to cut his hair—leaving it long in the front and close to the head in the back. I would cut it in the dining room of our apartment, while he sat in a chair, a hand towel draped around his shoulders. When I would shape his bangs, I'd often pause to kiss him on the lips, just before moving to the sides of his head, where I'd thin out the hair that sat over the arms of his glasses.

I am certain that he immediately drove home after the taping of the show so that we could watch it together. We would have been sitting on the turquoise futon in our living room in front of our hand-me-down TV. We'd be sipping on beers, high-fiving, and chain-smoking. He'd keep glancing over at me, looking for my approval as I stared at the screen, and then I'd pat his hands with giddy glee. He'd then point out that he played too fast and, even though I noticed it too, I'd kiss away his self-criticism and tell him it was just perfect. And then he'd say, with a glint of embarrassment in his tired, blue eyes: "Do you mind if I watch it again?" And I'd laugh at him and say: "OF COURSE NOT, DUMMY!"

And now, I must stop the clip and close my browser, because I'm suddenly overwhelmed with the memory of how good we once were—a fact I don't allow myself to indulge, because it hurts too much. Because I don't know that boy anymore. Or that girl, for that matter.

So, instead, I try to remind myself of who we are now and why it's best that we are over. I think about the day he asked me for a divorce. August 4, 2009. Just two days earlier, I had left for Warsaw, Poland, on a two-month research trip for a book I was writing. It was one of the few times in our relationship that I had done the leaving. I always feared that if we were both bouncing around the world for the sake of our careers, we'd never last.

Right before our phone conversation, I was awoken from a nap by a nasty dream. That's when I called him, the chalky taste of afternoon sleep still in my mouth. And that is when he said, in so many words, that he didn't want to be with me anymore.

"You mean, you want a divorce?" I asked.

As I sat there waiting for his answer, an ocean between us, I rubbed the cracked letters of the Tin Huey T-shirt into my chest, like salve into a wound, my worst nightmare before me.

2. A silk-screened poster from the September 22, 2000, Mary Timony concert in Oberlin, Ohio.

I was 19 when we first started dating. Patrick was 20, just six months older. We had known each other since our sophomore year in high school. He was tall and lanky, with pockmarked skin and thick black-rimmed glasses. "An indie rock Abraham Lincoln" is how a friend once described him. We made a comical pair. I was half his size, though my face was just as long and angular. I was just as frenetic and mouthy.

It was one of the best summers I have ever had. We bought matching seventies roller skates from the thrift store and rode around parking lots late at night, his car stereo blasting Thin Lizzy or Pavement. We'd sneak into bars and order cocktails like sloe gin fizzes and Rumple Minze and then dance around like maniacs. We agreed that we were soul mates because we both loved coconut cream pie, salami with mustard, and Camel Lights soft packs. We made paintings, mixed tapes, and fanzines, and planned for a future in which we'd always be doing that: making things together. We even started our own little band, just the two of us, sitting in his bedroom, writing silly pop songs about Vespas that we'd then record onto his four-track. In August, when I had to go back to Oberlin, Patrick cried. He didn't want me to go.

It was when he was up on one of his usual visits that we got word Mary Timony would be playing a show on campus. She was the reigning queen of indie rock, the former lead singer of Helium, who'd written one of our favorite songs, "Pat's Trick." "We should try to get on that show!" Patrick said. I handed the show organizers a tape of our songs and that was it. We were the opening act for one of our favorite musicians ever. That's how it always worked with Patrick. He always did what he said he was gonna do.

Patrick named our band Churchbuilder—a bizarre and esoteric reference to *The Eyes of Tammy Faye*, one of his favorite movies at the time. Unfortunately, we soon realized the limitations of my musical skills. For me, singing and playing keyboards proved as challenging as discrete math. Our little duo wouldn't be able to pull it off without help. We quickly recruited a couple of friends to perform with us. We taught them the very simple structures of our four modest songs and then, together, learned how to play "Tugboat" by Galaxie 500 as the final number. Five songs, 20 or so minutes. That would have to do.

That night at the student union, somewhere between the second and third song, I realized that I was enjoying myself. There was a rush to being onstage, having people cheer you on, stare up at you from the crowd like that, laughing at your stage banter. And then, after the show, strangers coming up to you, wanting to get to know you, genuinely excited to talk to you.

After that show, Churchbuilder continued for a bit longer. A small indie label out of Brooklyn, N.Y., put out our record, *Patty Darling*. We played a handful of gigs throughout the Midwest and the East Coast. We were lucky if ten people showed up, but we never cared. At least, I didn't. I had no designs on being a rock star. I wanted to be an academic, maybe a writer. But it was different for Patrick.

At the time, Patrick also began a project with a guy named Dan Auerbach. Dan and Pat had played music a couple of times in high school. I knew Dan because he lived across the street from my ex-boyfriend. Dan was a soccer jock who idolized Dave Matthews and G. Love and Special Sauce. Bands I despised. He was a real macho type who walked around town like a bulldog. He listened to Howard Stern, called his girlfriends "babe" and referred to indie pop as "gay." I never did like Dan much. And I know he never liked me. He and Patrick were complete opposites with little in common except for one thing: insatiable ambition.

We kept little evidence of our time in Churchbuilder. I think its existence embarrassed Patrick once the Black Keys catapulted onto the A-list of gritty, serious rock bands. For Christmas one year, I framed the poster from the Mary Timony show along with a dozen Black Keys ones as his present. It ended up on the second floor of our house, in my office.

3. "Crazy Rhythms" by the Feelies (on white vinyl)

In the early days of the Black Keys, Dan's girlfriend, Tarrah, and I would accompany Dan and Pat on tour, not because it was such great fun, but because that was the only way we could ever see them. It would be the four of us, piled into Pat's baby blue Plymouth Voyager minivan that stunk of boys. Tarrah and I would help load equipment in and out of clubs, drive and sell merchandise at shows.

During one of the more grueling tours, the band played a show in Athens, Ga. Directly next to the venue was a record store that specialized in rare records. On the wall, they displayed a copy of the Feelies' *Crazy Rhythms* in white vinyl.

Patrick and I were huge fans of the Feelies—tragic pop songwriters from the late eighties who gave up rock stardom for quieter lives. We particularly liked listening to them in the spring, while we sat out on the porch and pounded Belgian beer. The store was selling the record for $25. When Patrick saw the price tag, his face dropped. We couldn't justify spending that much. He shrugged and walked next door for sound check.

I stepped out of the store for a quick second to think. I lit a cigarette and rummaged through my bag for a bank receipt. My checking account balance: $14.28.

At the time, I had one credit card. A Discover card, no less. It had a $200 limit. About $50 of that was left. But the store wouldn't take credit. I went to an ATM and promptly withdrew what was left on the card, wincing at the thought of the inflated interest rate on such a cash advance. I then headed back to the store and bought the record.

After sound check, I gave it to Pat. His eyes almost bugged out of his head with guilt and gratitude. "But we can't afford this," he said. I just smiled.

In the end, when it came to dividing our 500 records, we didn't really fight. He told me to take what I wanted and leave the rest. I tried to be fair and remember exactly what I had brought into the relationship and what I had acquired, personally, during it. Bikini Kill's *Pussy Whipped* and Nico's *Chelsea Girl* were no-brainers, as were almost all of the bebop records that I had purchased during a "jazz" phase. He could keep the John Cale. And though I wanted to take Nick Drake's *Bryter Layter*, it had belonged to his father originally.

The Feelies was the toughest to decide upon. Sure, I'd bought it for him. But there was so little for me to recover of what I gave that relationship. Most of my giving was immaterial. The Feelies record was the only tangible memory of my sacrifice, some physical evidence of my dedication.

A few days after I'd split up our records, he sent me an e-mail. "Did you take that Feelies record? I really want it. It has special memories for me," he wrote. "You bought it for me when we had no money."

"Exactly," I wrote back.

4. A big-ass dining room table

The day I went to our old house to separate records, I also had to place Post-it notes on every piece of furniture I wanted to take with me. The Post-it notes were his idea. He also told me to take anything we'd acquired as a wedding present, including the dining room table that we'd purchased with a gift certificate from one of his relatives. Funny, since I was probably the least ecstatic by the prospect of marriage in the first place.

Two years into our relationship, my parents got divorced. It was a nasty, protracted legal battle. By the time they finally signed the papers in 2005, my mother was basically homeless, my brother had suffered a nervous breakdown, and I found myself at the start of a drinking problem. As for my father, he ran off with another woman to Santiago, Chile, to begin a new life. A fan of marriage, I was not.

Still, when Patrick proposed, I said yes, because what girl would be dumb enough to refuse a marriage offer from the love of her life? Plus, we'd been together six years already and it seemed like the logical next step in a relationship I'd completely built my life around.

We were in Chicago when he did it. He was playing two shows there that weekend. He got us an extra-fancy room at a nice downtown hotel—something really contemporary and swank with expensive lighting. We probably looked pretty goofy in that room, in our secondhand clothes that stunk of cigarette smoke. We over-tipped the staff, a gesture that begged: "Thanks for not kicking us out." It was a far cry from the literally bloodied mattresses of the trucker motels in which we used to sleep.

He opened a bottle of champagne, while I lit a cigarette. He tried to get into a kneeling position, but, at 6-foot-4 inches, he was too tall to do it gracefully. Finally, he gave up, pulled a vintage diamond ring in a simple platinum setting from the chest pocket of his plaid thrift store shirt and asked me to marry him.

I acted as excited as I could, throwing my arms around him and then admiring the ring for as long as I figured any happy bride-to-be would. But inside, I was terrified. I wanted more than anything to *want* to be married to him. But it felt awkward—like us in that fancy room. I suggested that we elope, but he said no, he wanted a proper wedding with all of our friends and family present. And that made me even more nervous.

When our wedding day came, my side of the chapel was sorely empty of relatives. My father didn't come, nor did any of his family.

Not a single cousin, aunt or grandparent. My brother gave me away in front of my grandmother and my mother. And that was it for family. I made sure to get very drunk before walking down the aisle in order to numb the pain of their absence.

If someone deserved all of our wedding presents, it was Patrick's mother, Mary. In fact, it was Mary who planted the seed of marriage in Patrick's mind.

Just a few weeks before he purchased a ring, Mary took him out to dinner. She asked him why he hadn't proposed marriage yet and if it had to do with the fact that she and his dad had gotten divorced. She told him it was unfair to his entire family for him not to propose to me—because they loved me and didn't want to lose me.

In many ways, the most enticing prospect of marrying Pat was belonging to his family. Despite their divorce, Patrick's parents managed to overcome their grievances. It was at our house that they celebrated their first Thanksgiving together in almost twenty years—Jim and his wife, Katie; Mary and her husband, Barry. Soon, we were all vacationing together like one big, happy family.

It only seemed fitting then, that I used the largest Target gift certificate we received to buy something my new family would appreciate. I figured a large dining room table would do. It was rectangular and sturdy and could accommodate up to ten people, eight comfortably. Before our marriage, I often hosted dinner parties for Patrick's family. They'd scatter about, balancing plates on knees, or eating standing up in the kitchen. Now, we could finally put them all at one table.

In the end, what hurt more than Patrick's request for a divorce was his mother's enthusiasm for one. In fact, it was a voice mail she left for him that signaled the end for me. I heard the message while I was sitting in my room in Poland, just after Patrick and I had talked about how he wasn't happy. I needed to know why. It wasn't my message to hear, but my respect for boundaries had been trumped by growing paranoia. She'd called to leave him the number of domestic court judges and divorce attorneys. "If you get a dissolution it will only take 90 days and if she's difficult, something like nine months. Well, that's it. Off to a girls' night out! Love ya! Bye!"

I can still hear the chipper tone of her voice in my head—the nasal, Midwestern perkiness. It still makes my stomach turn to think of how complicit she was in all of it and how easy she made it seem to dispose of me.

As for the table: Whenever I look at it, I resent how much space it takes up. But I don't want to sell it or give it away, because I never want to have to buy another like it again.

5. The Futon

Shortly after I moved all of my things out of our house, Patrick called. "Hey, could you also take the futon in the spare bedroom?" he said flatly. "I don't want it."

His request stung. It made me feel embarrassed and dirty. Because I knew exactly why he wanted me to take it.

We had spent a good chunk of our relationship on that futon. When I was at Oberlin, Patrick moved it into my dorm room so that we wouldn't have to sleep on the super narrow, extra-long twin provided by the school. After college, when I first moved in with Patrick, it served as our living room couch, until we finally bought a real sofa, and it began serving as our guest room bed.

By that time, Patrick was constantly on tour. I knew he was leaving because he had to. These were opportunities not to be missed. But that didn't make it feel any better. I tried to keep busy with my job as a newspaper reporter. But mostly, I was sad and lonely. I started drinking by myself. I'd get good and drunk and then I'd call Patrick, crying and screaming. The next morning, I'd wake up with dread over my behavior, call him back, and apologize profusely. "You've gotta stop doing this," he'd say.

"I know," I'd respond. "It's just so hard sometimes."

"It's hard for me, too."

I never knew how to fix it. Then, I made it worse. It was the fall of 2004. I did not love the man I brought home, to our futon. That is not why I did it. I did it because I was furious for being left behind and scared of what Patrick could do to hurt me—the sort of thing my dad did and the things Dan was doing to his girlfriend while she waited for him at home, putting her life on hold, just like me. I was a fool if I didn't think Patrick was doing the same thing—even if I had no proof. I wasn't that special.

I remember sitting on the couch the next morning, nursing a 12-pack of Pabst to stop the shaking, thinking of what to do. I decided not to tell Patrick. It would devastate him. Instead, I decided to move out and dry out for a bit. I couldn't be a tour widow anymore. It was killing me.

A week later, I moved out. It was the week before I started a new job, the weekend of my 23rd birthday. Patrick wasn't home from tour yet. I had a few girlfriends help me lug the awkward futon down the back steps of our building and move my stuff just a couple of blocks away to a small efficiency apartment. I also started going to therapy, where I was diagnosed with alcohol-induced mood disorder, a diagnosis that I quickly dismissed because I thought I knew better. I thought, "I don't have problems because I drink. I drink because I have problems."

Patrick blamed himself, for all the touring, all the things he'd asked me to give up. He'd make it up to me, he promised. He'd show me how much I mattered to him. He'd stop touring so much, he'd say. Six months later, I moved back in with him, lugging my secret behind me.

Of course, nothing really changed, because nothing really does. Patrick started touring even more. I started drinking even more. And our fights only grew worse. There was beer thrown. I put a fist through a window. We crashed on the floors of friends' houses after long, drunken battles that would carry on into the wee hours of the morning. Our friends started to believe it was simply our strange form of foreplay.

Then, one night, I couldn't keep it in anymore. It should have been an idyllic night. Pat was home from tour. We'd just spent the day grocery shopping and setting up our Christmas tree. It was only four months after we'd gotten married. *Things were supposed to be different.* "Patrick," I said. "I have to tell you something."

I was extremely drunk when I made my confession, so I don't remember specific details. I know that I slept at a friend's house that night and that, when I returned the next day, shards of Christmas tree decorations were strewn across the living room floor. Patrick was nowhere to be found. I immediately walked upstairs and collapsed into our bed. I felt I had just ruined the most important part of my life.

Patrick tried to forgive me and we tried to move on, but we couldn't. The last year and a half of our marriage was dark and angry. Even after the divorce, I never could forgive myself for my infidelity. And the pages of the May 27, 2010, issue of *Rolling Stone* proved he couldn't either.

Then, one night, almost a year after we split up, Patrick called me. He sounded very drunk. And that's when he finally admitted that'd he also been unfaithful to me. Not just with the woman he'd left me for, but before that, even. One time, he said, on tour. He swore that it wasn't sex, just a bit of friendly fellatio, because, you know, he loved me so much he could never go all the way. "I swear that was the only time," he said. Oddly enough, I wasn't angry. I think I laughed. I was also glad that I didn't take the stupid futon, like he'd asked.

6. One audio MiniDisc of the Black Keys' first live performance, July 2002

This audio MiniDisc is a recording I made of the Black Keys. It is their first concert ever. I was one of only five people in attendance. I remember calling our friends and bribing them with shots to come and watch. The show was at the Beachland Tavern in Cleveland, Ohio, a cozy old man bar with Schlitz signs, $1 cans of Tecate, and a small stage that still plays host to a number of random garage bands, some that go on to great fame (the White Stripes) and some that don't (Churchbuilder). Since then, the Black Keys are much too popular to play the Tavern. They are now on the covers of magazines and win things like Grammy Awards.

For that reason, the MiniDisc could be valuable. I could sell it. I know there are some crazy fans out there who'd probably pay several hundred if I put it on eBay. Though, I'm not sure if the dissolution agreement would acknowledge it as my intellectual property or his. Legally, the MiniDisc probably belongs to him. His lawyers brilliantly made sure I had no claim to his musical legacy, despite helping build it. Nothing was said of my intellectual property in the dissolution agreement. It was as though I made nothing of value in our marriage—nothing important enough to protect with legalese, at least. Still, I signed the dotted line.

But I don't hold onto the recording for its monetary value. I hold it hostage for a sense of what's possible. I keep it so that I can throw it away. I hold onto it because Patrick knows I have it and he likes to think in terms of monetary value. I would like to see if he sues me for it, because then that would prove that he is truly the monster I think he's become—the monster I envision in my mind so that I will not love him anymore. I hold onto it with the idea that one day, I can mail it to his father, along with a 3×5 index card that says, "I thought you should have this." His father is a gentle man, and would be touched by my gesture, I'm sure. He loves memories. I think he still loves me. Also, if I sent it to Patrick's father, it would prove that I'm not greedy, unlike his son. The danger in sending it is that his father will give it to Patrick and then I will have no more power. I will have completely surrendered.

Mostly, though, I hold onto it because it is a beautiful and a horrible memory cast in sound. It was the beginning of something special. It was also the beginning of our end.

7. One black-and-white photo of Patrick and me, taken in 2003, at Apple Studios

In the year that Patrick and I have been divorced, I have taken to throwing a lot of mementos away—notes I'd hung onto, photos of him as a child, photos of us together, mix CDs he'd made me, our wedding invitations, wedding cards, backstage passes from shows, anything with the words "The Black Keys" on it.

It is entirely against my nature to destroy evidence. I usually hold onto relics of the past with obsessive zeal. Each purging was painful. But people told me that I had to let go, and so I took them literally, and tried to put what was left of us in the trash.

We didn't have a ton of printed photographs of ourselves together. In fact, there were precisely three that hung in our house. One was of us kissing on our wedding day. The other two were almost exactly alike: us, in black-and-white, in front of the Abbey Road Studios in London.

The first photo was taken in the summer of 2003. Our friend Ben Corrigan took it. In it, we are both flashing genuine smiles in front of a wall filled with Beatles-inspired graffiti. I can tell we are having fun. Life is still an adventure. I might be hung over, but I'm muscling my way through, as I could only do at 22. Patrick is thin and handsome. His hair is long. I'm wearing some insane Hawaiian dress and a calculator watch. His hand is holding my hands, which are rested on his knee. A few months after it was taken, Ben had it made into a postcard that he then sent from London. He wrote, "I love you crazy bitches!" on the back. It was one of the greatest surprises I've ever received in the mail.

The second photo was taken five years later. This time, we actually got to go inside Abbey Studios, because the Black Keys were doing a *Live From Abbey Road* session. I thought it would be fun if Ben took the same photo of us before we left.

Unfortunately, it was freezing outside and we were in a rush to the venue where the Black Keys were performing that night. Patrick seemed resistant, but I promised it would be fun, so he begrudgingly went along with it. Ben e-mailed it to me soon after we got back. In it, we are all in black. Patrick isn't smiling, but wincing. Our bodies are turned into each other, but it feels so forced. If you set the two photos next to each other, it was so painfully obvious that we'd grown apart.

The day I moved out, I wasn't going to take any photos with me. But then I thought: What if, one day, I have a daughter? Will I have to tell her that I was once married to a man she will never know, but who was one of the most important people in my life? That I was once madly in love with a man who isn't her father, but with whom I wanted to have children? Would I then need to show her some evidence of this relationship?

And then, I thought: This is the picture I will show her, an example that things were not always so sad and heavy. In fact, they were wonderful once.

BOMBING RUN

By Kyle Cochrun

The posse crept along Exchange Street around 3 a.m. one chilly Friday night in November of 2012, slinking under the highway before cutting over to Annadale Avenue. Annadale is one of ugliest backstreets near the University of Akron, where we all went to school. The sign on the corner is bent crooked, signifying the dejected state of the street, with its brick warehouse buildings marked in amateur graffiti, an open lot of tall weeds and a row of tattered college houses thrown on the end of the block. Devito lived in one of these houses at the time, and he picked our spot to tag that night: a dejected factory halfway down the road.

The backside of the building, a mess of brickwork, pipes, shattered glass, and dark crimson rust, faces Annadale, complementing the street's shabby character. It was the leftover carcass of one of the city's manufacturing plants, a great spot to bomb. We trekked under the streetlights with our clinking bags full of canisters toward the wreckage.

This had been my idea. My fascination with graffiti had grown parallel to my teenage infatuation with hip hop. To be a graffiti artist was to be a streetwise bandit concerned with aesthetics, to be a ghost wandering through subway tunnels, a silhouette straddling brick high-rises, looming over the cityscape and imprinting art into the concrete fabric of the world. It was also illegal and possibly dangerous, which was invigorating. In short, graffiti was an outlet of expression for my nineteen-year-old self and a chance to explore the degenerate city blocks my semi-sheltered suburban mind was drawn to.

My first tagging experience was sponsored by the nearest colossal superstore, which happened to be Walmart. I stopped in with my friend Mac and bought generic brand spray-paint canisters for a few bucks each. Mac had vandalized the suburbs with me in high school and would naturally be tagging along for my new felonious hobby.

A house party erupted that night at Mac's college house on Rankin Street, so I waited around for him to sober up enough to go out, impatiently wandering in and out of cliques of wasted college kids. He was far from sober, but finally gave in. Devito came along; he'd gone to high school with us and hung around in the summer, playing ultimate Frisbee with the crew. He'd also tagged before, making him our de facto graffiti captain. We also enlisted Ray "Boom Boom" Zielinski, Mac's college neighbor from Medina, a quiet kid with a sweet tooth for raw spots.

Our gang of white, middle-class kids stumbled out of the dying party and set off across the pavement in beanies and dark hoodies, searching out visceral fun amongst the industrial wreckage of our college city.

We faced the factory. A concrete bridge only wide enough for one person to cross at a time ran upwards from a field of weeds and over the street to the roof of a shorter section of the building. This was our only entrance, aside from finding a way to climb the barbed-wire fence. We hoisted each other up, shoes scraping the edge of the concrete, searching for traction. We made it up and crept across the bridge in a line, knees bent, towards the towering factory. Lights are scarce on Annadale, but a light pole loomed over us on both sides. I could feel small pebbles crushing under my sneakers.

Police sirens faded in to our right, blaring towards us. Then came flashing lights, reflecting blue and red off brick surfaces and overgrown trees forcing leaves through fences. We dropped to our chests and pressed cheeks to hard concrete as a police cruiser flew down the road. It passed underneath us, then off into the distance. We darted back up and headed for the roof. Nobody could see us from the street, right? Of course they could, but no one would look up. At least we hoped.

At the end of the bridge was a metal walkway that had rusted through and collapsed down on one side, leaving a strip of steel wide enough to balance on with one foot while carefully swinging the other foot directly in front to keep moving. This connected to a fire escape that led up to the pinnacle of the factory, a rectangular tower of corroding maroon steel.

We each went across, clinging to a rusty metal bar near our arms. If the strip below gave out and crashed downward, we could grip this bar, putting all our weight on it as our legs swung through the air, hoping it wouldn't break off too. There was a large, circular hole torn out of the steel roof underneath us, as if some large missile-like object had burst its way through. I peered inside to see where the floor was, but stared into blackness. It looked like an endless void which one of us might fall through forever.

I edged across the strip, filled with the sensation of mortal danger. I was just a misstep from falling to my death. How often does someone end up in this situation? This was a fierce amplification of the thrill I'd get in high school running from cars I'd left spattered in egg yolk and leaving trees streaked in glorious shrouds of toilet paper, anticipating a car pulling out of the garage for a getaway chase. Late-night suburban shenanigans were stale and gutless compared to the fear of inching across elevated, unstable rust. This was acute adventurous terror.

We made it across one at a time, offering a hand from the end of the platform to whoever was next, then hiked to the top of the staircase and opened a door, revealing a narrow room with a ceiling that shot up to the top of the building where we stood. There was no staircase inside for us to take down to the heart of the abandoned plant, just walls that disappeared downward on all sides into the abyss. We shut the door and brought out the cans, searching for a good surface to tag.

The metal walls were caked in rust, making white our paint color of choice. The ridges on the surface made it hard to spray straight lines and gave our basic tags a shambolic look. I made three-dimensional cubes with vertical lines for eyes and a slanted line for a mouth, giving it an adorably awkward grin. Devito tagged "Vito," filling in the bubble letters with color. We could tell he'd done this at least a few times before and we respected his limited skill.

"Nah dude, this is amateur shit," he said. I didn't care; the rush was great. We were actually creating something, adding to the myth of the landscape.

Mac scribbled slang terms we used as inside jokes, like "Legit Pro" and "Swag." Ray was only capable of making a messy portrait of Mickey Mouse, which everyone admired, even though I was hard-pressed to make out Mickey in the snaky lines.

Cans of spray paint hissed in the night air over the sounds of sirens in the distance. The streets were coming down from a wild night; kids stumbled on the sidewalk in groups of two, their voices echoing off the buildings under us. The shifting lights of a large electronic billboard hovering in the distance caused me to jolt my head sideways, nervous of more bright headlights coming our way. A few more police cruisers sped down the road, compelling us to crouch on the staircase and attempt to blend our black clothes in with the rust all around us. This became a regular occurrence until we eventually stopped caring and kept spraying our novice master-pieces as the cars zoomed by underneath.

We stepped back over the rail and crept over the concrete block, one after another, leaping back to the ground. Jordan squeezed his way over the barbed-wire to tag the wall of the building while Mac, Ray and I bombed a metal barrier that butted against the sidewalk. Satisfied for the night, we disappeared from under the streetlights and made our way past the rubble.

I jogged to the building the next morning, triumphant to see our novice artwork alive on the surface of this real-life relic. There was my box man, the black ink from his lines trickling down the wall. There was "Legit Pro" and "Vito" and Mickey (I still couldn't make out the mouse in the daylight). Our gallery was a scattered mess of clumsy tags, but it was complete, forever recording an eventful night in our young lives.

After this, I rarely acknowledged our exhibit on Annadale, and neither did the rest of the crew. Occasionally while passing on the highway, I could just barely make out our squiggly figures on the wall of the highest tower.

A month later I sat in the passenger seat of my dad's Camry as we chugged up Cuyahoga Street on our daily commute from suburbia to downtown Akron. A blip of radio bulletin on 1590 WAKR, the local AM radio station we tuned into most mornings, broke me out of a thoughtless lull.

"... Kent State student died last night after falling from the roof of the former Atlantic Foundry building on Annadale..."

I knew immediately that this was the building we'd tagged, without having known its name from a past lifetime. No other structure on the street was worthy of holding the final moments of a young urban explorer. There was only one memorable shell of a building on Annadale, and this had to be it.

"The old Atlantic Foundry. I know where that is," my dad said in a tone of some distant familiarity. "That's been closed for years."

He recalled a brief history of the foundry as he remembered it while I sat attentive, hoping to discover the significance this place once held, to learn more about the abyss I couldn't see into, without admitting to being a vandal.

The Atlantic Foundry Company was an iron casting business started in 1905 by a group of immigrants who were apparently inspired to name their company after the ocean they had crossed to come to America. They built their iron foundry between Beaver Street and Annadale Avenue in 1910, adding a steel foundry to the site in 1919. At one time, the company had 450 employees and its own credit union. In January of 1989 the foundry was shut down, becoming another site among the remnants of Akron's industrial days. A great spot to bomb. A great spot to explore.

The crew passed around an iPad in Mac's bedroom on Rankin. An article had been published in the *Akron Beacon Journal* on the death of the girl and had been posted on their website. Adrienne Ryba, a nineteen-year-old Kent State student, had stood on the roof with her boyfriend and another couple when her section gave out. She plunged through the hole into the abyss, which descended 40 or 50 feet.

Adrienne, her boyfriend, and the other young couple scaled their way to the roof over the concrete walkway just as we had. When Adrienne fell through, her boyfriend, frantic in the moment, came close to plunging himself through the hole.

"It happened fast and he couldn't catch her. They said they had to hold him back or he would have gone in after her," Adrienne's mother said. "They wanted to see the lights of the city and the meteor shower. Teenagers do crazy things like that. You think you're invincible when you're a teenager."

Our eyes were focused mostly on the pictures that accompanied the article. "Legit Pro" was almost perfectly legible in the shot of the rusty tower we had climbed. Apparently a section of the building had been bought out and was being used at the time for the production of machine knives for the plastic industry, adding a new shade of criminality to our exploit.

"Theirs was not a new idea; others had been there before them, as graffiti was sprayed on the side of the building," the article read.

That was us. We had been immortalized in the local paper as nameless criminals who had risked death to write some shitty scribbles that could never pass as art on the walls of a factory. And we were ecstatic about it. Our work had been displayed in condensed pixilated form to the world, with written attribution. A girl had lost her life for this moment; we understood the seriousness of this. But the details of her life: the fact that she and her boyfriend were high school sweethearts with plans for the future, her passion for art and volleyball, her dream to own an interior design studio; none of that seemed to touch us.

Now that some years have passed, I find myself imagining what the final seconds of her life might have been like. I picture the metal footing cracking underneath, then a sudden jolt into darkness. She catches a glimpse of night sky through the slit above and sees her friends looking down on her, their faces obscured. Then there is a thud as her skull strikes wet concrete.

The image is terrifying, and so is the fact that it could have been one of my friends, or myself, falling through the rust. Hadn't we wanted to be terrified, though? Wasn't that part of the thrill? It was for me, and I imagine it would have to be for any teenager willing to tread the brittle surface of a corroding building. Two groups of friends had used the foundry as a playground. We all wanted a visceral experience: a violent scare, the rush of breaking laws, a beautiful moment gazing into space from four stories up, the exhilaration of creating something from disused space. The thrill was worth the danger until the rust gave out on Adrienne. Seconds after she fell through the roof and smacked the ground her friends must have realized that we are all doomed, sometimes at random, and should respect our mortality. I think a weaker version of that same realization was unconsciously planted in the minds of my friends and me as we stood in that bedroom reading the article aloud and flicking through the photographs. It wasn't enough to kill our urge to blend danger with fun, but it was there.

I jogged by the factory one morning a few weeks later. Our tags had been removed, covered over with white blotches of paint. No one would know we had been there, just that some punks had sprayed something on the building that was doomed to be concealed from the eyes of passersby. I stood there, disappointed, staring up at the relic now returned to its pure state.

I believe that one night in the future, if it hasn't happened already, another clique of college students, fascinated by the legend of Adrienne Ryba's death and the mystery of the foundry, will scuffle across the concrete block and climb the stairs of the tower to gaze into the abyss from which she never returned. The cycle will continue. As the factory rests, myth pervades its existence.

THERE'S NO PLACE LIKE HOME

By Emilia Sykes

Sitting in the open conference room, blue walls, clean edges, and a dog, my life spread across the table. Who am I? What do I do? Why am I here? The table was filled with old photos, awards, and a lifetime of memories—events that developed and shaped a young and growing politico. Medals from gymnastics competitions, photos of dance recitals, middle, high, college, and law school graduation, family portraits, all filled with a sense of accomplishment, love, and hope. This discussion changed from nostalgia to the future. "What do you see as the message of the campaign?"

"There's no place like home," I replied.

As a college freshman, I grew restless in Northeast Ohio. I knew that there was a larger world out there and I wanted to explore it. The notion of that was easier said than done, though, and sent me on a quest to find an opportunity to leave the community I called home for an adventure. I found a student exchange program that would allow me to explore another university and community then come back to Kent State a year later. The next semester I left for rural Alabama. I came back home two years later.

The Wizard of Oz was my favorite movie as a child. I don't know why I was so drawn to the film but I loved everything about it. Maybe it was the colors, the songs, the dancing, whatever it was, I watched the VHS more times that I could humanly count. And when I was introduced to the *The Wiz*, an African-American remake starring Michael Jackson and Diana Ross, I was a fan forever. Little did I know that the plot of those movies would be become my story. A story about a young girl wanting more, an adventure, looking for a place to grow and thrive. Traveling to distant lands, picking up new friends and problems along the way, facing adversity and ultimately having to believe in yourself in order to find your way to the place where you belonged.

In *The Wizard of Oz*, Judy Garland as Dorothy sings about a place "somewhere over the rainbow." A place where the dreams that you dreamed of come true and where "troubles melt like lemondrops." That's where you would find her and that's where I wanted to go too.

My "somewhere over the rainbow" led me to Alabama, Italy,

Georgia, Florida, and Georgia, again.

Each of the places I visited had their own challenges and opportunities. All of these places welcomed me as one of their own, but I wasn't. I was an Akronite, no matter how far I had traveled. I often found myself sharing little-known Akron facts, and every time the opportunity presented itself, I would acknowledge an invention, a person, a historical event that had a connection to the city. Referring to carbonated beverages as "pop" and the grassy area between the sidewalk and the street as a "devil strip" I was always connected to the city of Akron even though physically I was hundreds of miles away.

For many people who've grown up in tough and difficult situations, home is not a place they ever want to go back to. I didn't have that experience; home was a refuge and it was clear by the many pit stops I took back to Akron in between my re-locations over the years. Each return serving as an opportunity to prepare for the next adventure. But after a while I didn't feel the need to search for a new place to go because I already had a home, one that was waiting for me to return whenever I was ready.

I once heard a story during a panel on families where a community leader told a story about her grandchildren moving to another state. The children questioned where their home would be since they would no longer be in the place where they were born. The response was home is where your family is and where you feel most loved. For me, Akron is home—where my family is, where I'm most comfortable, where I feel most loved.

When I ran for State Representative, I wanted my campaign to encompass the journey I had taken back home. I had come to appreciate the city of Akron in a way that I never had before. I felt the need to share the story exactly how I came to understand it. This city has given so much to me, and it was time for me to give back to the place that has helped mold me into who I am today. The way for me to do that was to take all that I had learned in my travels, education and experience, and become a public servant in my hometown for the people of Akron. I felt, and I still feel as though I have a responsibility to make sure that Akron remains a great place to call home. Not just for those born and raised here but also for those who feel the most love when they are here. The magnitude of explaining the feeling became overwhelming at times and caused a few emotional moments on the campaign trail. But through the occasional cracking voice, I was hopeful that I could resonate through my message why I wanted to be here, serve and would rather be here than any other place in the world.

After many years of trying to find my way and my place, I never had to look any further than what was right inside of me the entire time. I no longer felt like Dorothy, looking for somewhere over the rainbow. I identify much more with Dorothy played by Diana Ross who famously sang, "When I think of home, I think of a place where there's love overflowing." That place has always been Akron, Ohio, for me and I am glad to call it home.

HAIL TO THE KING

By Matt Stansberry

I was born in Akron. My deathbed request for a final meal would be a Swenson's Galley Boy, and I'd wash it down with a California. My grandfather retired from the Firestone Tire Factory, and as a kid I worked for Goodyear doing park maintenance at Wingfoot Lake. My mom graduated from Akron Public Schools and Akron University, and taught Special Education in those same city schools.

I know almost nothing about basketball. But I can speak to you as a son of Akron.

LeBron James. I write his name over and over. I say the words like a prayer in the silence of my kitchen, the day after LeBron won it all for us.

In my view, never in professional sports has an athlete meant so much to a city.

In his now-famous "Nothing is given" *Sports Illustrated* essay, James wrote:

Before anyone ever cared where I would play basketball, I was a kid from Northeast Ohio. It's where I walked. It's where I ran. It's where I cried. It's where I bled. It holds a special place in my heart. People there have seen me grow up. I sometimes feel like I'm their son.

In July 2014, I was at my aunt's house in Portage Lakes on the Friday afternoon that LeBron James announced his return to Ohio. I heard a radio from somewhere nearby, not even the words, just excitement in the announcers' voices carrying over the water, and I knew what had happened.

I rolled in the grass and screamed in joy. My aunt tried to explain to my very young sons what was happening to their father. But again, I don't love basketball or the Cavaliers. I love LeBron James.

On June 19, 2016, James led the Cleveland Cavaliers to an unprecedented come-from-behind win to snatch the NBA title from the much-favored Golden State Warriors. Through tears in the postgame interview, he said, "I don't know why we take the hardest road. . . I strive the most when everyone counts us out."

This is the Akron ethos, even more so than Cleveland or any other city.

There is no place more self-conscious than Northeast Ohio, a place with a chip on its shoulder.

When, in the postgame, James said "I understand what Northeast Ohio has been through the last fifty years," you knew it was the truth.

In the same breath, he said he kept the pressures of our hopes and expectations at bay these past two years, and you knew he was kidding himself.

Even as he executes superhuman feats of athleticism, you see him processing everything. You see it in the strain on his face and the new gray hair in his beard along his jawline.

When the Cleveland *Plain Dealer* headline in 2015 was "Not Enough Grit" I lost it. I wrote to the editors. I called and screamed like a lunatic at the unfortunate woman in customer service as I cancelled my subscription. We in Akron are fiercely protective.

When the shitheel critics complain about his relationship with the officials, or mock his hairline, his cramping legs, I feel a visceral pain and protectiveness, the way I would if someone had hurt my child.

But I am unnerved by the responsibility of what I feel I need to say here. I am not qualified to write about race. My privilege and upbringing do not disqualify me necessarily, but my lack of any depth or rigorous thinking on this subject do. I will try to do this next part justice.

Two of them men in the world I admire the most are young black guys with absent fathers.

In December of 2014, Barack Obama praised LeBron James for following in the path of Muhammad Ali toward raising racial consciousness by wearing a shirt during pregame warmups that read "I Can't Breathe," the last words of Eric Garner, an unarmed black man who died while in a police chokehold.

When asked about the shirt, LeBron said, "As a society we have to do better. We have to be better for one another no matter what race you are."

Everyone knows the story of LeBron James growing up in poverty in Akron and becoming the world's greatest sports icon. But the day after the championship was clinched, I spent time meditating on a photo I saw making the rounds on social media.

In this photo James is probably the same age as my oldest boy, wearing a cardigan and clutching a stuffed elephant.

This image of a vulnerable boy reminds me of a note I had read that LeBron wrote to the young kids of Akron earlier this year, the kids LeBron is working to get into college programs.

It's tough to get out of the bed in the morning when it's cold and dark. Sometimes, all I want to do is stay in bed and watch cartoons, so I know how it feels. No matter what, we have to get out of bed and go to work. Understood?

I hope you guys have an incredible week. You'll be on my mind, I PROMISE.

A lot of people argue that LeBron has a messiah complex, a state of mind in which an individual holds a belief that he or she is, or is destined to become a savior.

In most cases, the definition above relates to a delusion of grandeur, but in this case it is practical. LeBron's messiah complex is not that he's not going to save the world. He's saving Akron. He's saving us.

Contributors

David Giffels' books include *The Hard Way on Purpose: Essays and Dispatches From the Rust Belt* (Scribner 2014); *All the Way Home,* (William Morrow, 2008), *Are We Not Men? We Are Devo!* (co-written with Jade Dellinger, SAF Publishing 2003), and *Wheels of Fortune: The Story of Rubber in Akron* (co-written with Steve Love, University of Akron Press 2008). A former *Akron Beacon Journal* columnist, his writing has appeared in the *New York Times Magazine, Parade,* the *Wall Street Journal,* Esquire.com, Grantland.com, *Redbook,* and many other publications. He also was a writer for the MTV series *Beavis and Butt-Head.* He is an associate professor of English at University of Akron, where he teaches creative nonfiction in the Northeast Ohio Master of Fine Arts Program.

Pat Jarrett is a photographer and editor working in Virginia's Shenandoah Valley, but he was born and raised in and around Akron. Jarrett is married to a fire-breathing seamstress and prefers two-wheeled transportation to four any day of the week. He believes the low-and-slow method is best for cooking meat, luck is a manifestation of hard work, and daily newspaper photography is a surreal art form.

L.S. Quinn was raised in Northeast Ohio and has a B.A. in English from the University of Akron. She's worked in churches and social service agencies in Akron, Cleveland, and Chicago. After writing and performing in Chicago for more than a decade, she's come back to Akron to serve the Grace Park area. She loves slam poetry, vintage fashion, and Scrabble.

Greg Milo heads the Social Studies Department at Archbishop Hoban High School, where he teaches World Cultures, International Politics, and Hometown Histories. He also coordinates Hoban's Project HOPE program, guiding students each Wednesday evening to hang out with Akron's less fortunate brothers and sisters. He is a frequent contributor to the *Akronist* and has written articles for education journals, such as *Education Week.*

Matt Tullis is an associate professor of journalism at Ashland University and is the producer and host of Gangrey: The Podcast. He is also an associate editor of River Teeth, a journal of nonfiction. He has written for *SB Nation, Cleveland Magazine, Nieman Storyboard, Sports On Earth* and many others. He lives with his wife and two children on the edge of Amish country in Wayne County, Ohio.

Maria Mancinelli is a native of Cuyahoga Falls and a graduate of Miami University where she earned a Bachelors degree in International Studies and Latin American Studies in 2011. Maria began her career in Brazil as a Fulbright English Teaching Assistant at the Federal University of Uberlândia. She relocated to Akron in 2013 where she worked as Community Outreach Coordinator for the International Institute of Akron. Maria recently moved to Milan, Italy to better understand Europe's response to the current refugee crisis and hopes to begin graduate study in Europe in fall of 2016.

Roza Maille is an artist and arts administrator living in her adopted hometown of Akron, Ohio. She works for the Akron Art Museum, Artists of Rubber City, and is a big supporter of all things creative. Traveling is her number one hobby but she's always glad to come back home to her husband and two cats.

Jeff Shearl is a writer from Akron, Ohio, and a graduate of the university of Akron's English program. He has difficulty taking most things seriously, and as a result lives a life of excitement, intrigue, and mystery.

Andrew Poulsen is an Akron-born writer and musician currently living in Cleveland. Andrew is a graduate of the E.W. Scripps School of Journalism at Ohio University. He has written for Billboard.com, *Cleveland Magazine, Ohio Magazine* and several other regional and national publications. He is an avid enthusiast of U.S. history, the Cleveland Cavaliers and Fender guitars.

Jason Segedy is the Director of Planning and Urban Development for the City of Akron, Ohio. He has worked in the urban planning field for the past 21 years, and previously served as the Director of the Akron Metropolitan Area Transportation Study (AMATS), the Metropolitan Planning Organization serving Greater Akron. He is an avid writer on urban planning and development issues, blogging at Notes from the Underground. His work has been published by *Planetizen, Streetsblog, Rustwire, Wise Economy, Real Clear Policy,* and *New Geography.* A lifelong resident of Akron's west side, Jason is committed to the city, its people, and its neighborhoods. His passion is creating great places and spaces where residents can live, work, and play. He came into this world at St. Thomas Hospital, in 1972, and he'll continue to do this work until they put him in the ground at Holy Cross Cemetery—hopefully a long time from now.

Jennifer Conn is an Akron-based freelance reporter and writer. With her recent focus on life in Northeast Ohio, Jennifer's work has appeared in *The Devil Strip, Crain's' Akron Business and Crain's Cleveland Business.* As a daily news and trade reporter in Ohio and Kentucky, she's covered crime and the environment, as well as the automotive, tire and recycling industries. With an MA in journalism from Kent State University and a (nearly completed) post-graduate certificate in TESL, she also teaches English composition and English as a Second Language courses at KSU and the University of Akron. Jennifer's interest in cemeteries is an extension of her passion for honoring our historical sites and structures through storytelling.

Joanna Wilson is the author of *The Story of Archie the Talking Snowman & Akron's History of Christmas Attractions* (2015), and the co-author of *A is For Akron* (2014). She earns her living as a Christmas entertainment writer. In 2010, she wrote *Tis the Season TV: The Encyclopedia of Christmas-themed Episodes, Specials and Made-for-TV Movies,* an 800-page reference book with over 3000 listings which earned her national attention. She stays active as the Assistant Director of Crafty Mart, an organizer of *Dance Dance Party Party-Akron,* and a contributor to *Akron Empire* and the *Devil Strip.* Although she grew up in Cuyahoga Falls, she now lives in Highland Square where she counts herself as one of the area's many memorable characters.

Akron native **Rita Dove**, former U.S. Poet Laureate, is the recipient of numerous honors, including the Pulitzer Prize, the Heinz Award, the National Humanities Medal, and the National Medal of Arts. Her many books include the poetry collections *Thomas and Beulah, Sonata Mulattica, American Smooth,* and *On the Bus with Rosa Parks,* the novel *Through the Ivory Gate,* and the play *The Darker Face of the Earth.* Her *Collected Poems 1974-2004* will be published in 2016 by W.W. Norton. Dove is Commonwealth Professor of English at the University of Virginia.

Mike Gruss is a journalist who lives in Alexandria, Virginia. He covers national security issues related to space for the magazine *SpaceNews.* Previously, he worked as a columnist and reporter for The *Virginian-Pilot* newspaper in Norfolk, Virginia. He graduated from Miami University in Oxford, Ohio, and owns a T-shirt with the Route 8 logo printed on the front.

Originally from Portland, Oregon, **Eric Wasserman** is the author of a collection of short stories, *The Temporary Life,* and a novel, *Celluloid Strangers.* He is an Associate Professor of English at The University of Akron where he teaches creative writing, literature and film studies. He lives in Akron, Ohio with his wife, Thea. You can visit him at www.ericwasserman.com.

Patricia Fann was born in Akron and spent her earliest years in Akron's Kenmore area until the 1960's when I-277 was built, cutting through the neighborhood, and her parents moved to Manchester (or New Franklin as it's now called). She has lived with her husband in an older house in West Akron for 30 years, raising their three daughters.

Matthew Meduri teaches writing at Kent State University. A graduate of the NEOMFA program, his work has appeared in *Cactus Heart, Milk Sugar,* and *Rubbertop Review.* Although Matthew lives in Kent, Ohio, he is no stranger to the Rubber City, having spent a good majority of his adolescence seeing shows at the Lime Spider. He is currently working on a novel.

Liesl Schwabe's essays have appeared in *Salon, Publishers Weekly, Creative Nonfiction, Tricycle: The Buddhist Review,* and *The Common,* along with several other journals and anthologies. She currently directs the Writing Program at Yeshiva College and lives in Brooklyn, N.Y., with her husband and two children.

Chris Drabick is a former rock music journalist whose fiction has appeared in *Midwestern Gothic* and *Great Lakes Review,* and non-fiction in *BULL* and *Stoneboat.* He was the recipient of a 2012 Juniper Summer Fellowship, as well as winner of the Marion Smith Short Story Prize. He teaches English at the University of Akron, where he lives with his wife, their two sons, and too many vinyl LPs.

Denise Grollmus was a reporter at the *Cleveland Scene* (2004-2008) and the *Akron Beacon Journal* (2003-2004). In 2005, the Ohio Society of Professional Journalistsnamed her "Best Essayist in Ohio" and her work was anthologized in Best American Crime Writing 2006. Denise is now a writer, teacher, and scholar whose work has appeared in numerous publications, including *Salon, the Guardian, New York Magazine, Tablet,* and various *Village Voice* papers. She holds an MFA in Creative Writing from Penn State and was a Fulbright scholar to Poland. She is currently working on her PhD in English at the University of Washington in Seattle.

Kyle Cochrun is a first-year student in the NEOMFA creative writing program. He is obsessed with *American Graffiti* and hip-hop culture.

Born and raised in Akron, State Representative **Emilia Strong Sykes** was elected to represent her hometown in November 2014. As representative, Sykes has pushed an aggressive job creation plan, fighting to keep local jobs for local workers and expand opportunities for middle and working class families in Akron. Representative Sykes has also worked with healthcare professionals and colleagues to improve public health, increase access to care, and combat Ohio's high infant mortality rate. Her passion for social justice extends to issues such as voter rights, criminal justice reform, a more efficient social safety net for struggling Ohioans, and an end to domestic violence. Sykes attended Kent State University, graduating magna cum laude with a B.A. in Psychology. She later attended the University of Florida, where she earned a Juris Doctor with a Certificate in Family Law from the Levin College of Law and a Masters of Public Health from the College of Public Health and Health Professions. Representative Sykes serves as Ranking Member of the House Finance and Appropriations Subcommittee on Health and Human Services. She also serves on the House Finance and Appropriations Committee, House Judiciary Committee, House Ways and Means Committee, the Joint Medicaid Oversight Committee, and the Ohio Constitutional Modernization Committee.

Joanna Richards has been a reporter and editor for print weeklies, daily newspapers, and public radio outlets in Louisville, Kentucky; Watertown, New York; and Cleveland, Ohio. She was an assistant editor for the first book based on the revived personal essay radio series, *This I Believe.* Her radio work has aired nationally on NPR's hourly newscast *Morning Edition, Here and Now,* and *Marketplace.* Recently she's moved to freelance writing and editing, to make room for things she should have done in her twenties, like working on a farm, getting certified as a kayak guide, cycling and camping through hundreds of miles of Ontario with an exotic foreign love interest, and being poor. She lives in Cleveland with a parade of diverse roommates and visitors, both human and animal.